About This Book

MW00387254

Why is this topic important?

Trainers sometimes faii to ask enough questions or the right question prior to designing, redesigning, or presenting a training program as the solution to a problem. Then they find out during the training event, or just after it ends, that the training missed the mark. Even trainers who put together a training plan before reserving a classroom and rolling out a training program can run the risk of wasting resources and reaping unsatisfactory results. With economic pressure to cost-justify every training dollar, trainers need to have a clear objective for what training will accomplish and a specific plan for how to get there.

What can you achieve with this book?

This book provides models and tools to help trainers become more strategic and focused in their efforts so that greater results can be achieved. Go beyond the basics of asking a few questions by selecting the right type of needs analysis, conducting the needs analysis appropriately, and creating a training plan to sell to management on meeting a business need. Conserve precious resources by providing training only when it is needed.

How is this book organized?

Each chapter begins with objectives to help trainers and course designers identify what new skills and insights can move their needs assessment skills beyond the basics. Chapter tools, including models, examples, templates, and checklists, are provided in the accompanying CD for customizing and duplication. Each chapter begins with questions that guide the reader through the chapter contents. Finally, a chapter on how to summarize all the needs assessment data into a training plan completes the book. The reference section identifies the competencies with supporting knowledge, skills, and attitudes that a trainer or course designer needs to conduct various types of needs analysis and develop a training plan.

About Pfeiffer

Pfeiffer serves the professional development and hands-on resource needs of training and human resource practitioners and gives them products to do their jobs better. We deliver proven ideas and solutions from experts in HR development and HR management, and we offer effective and customizable tools to improve workplace performance. From novice to seasoned professional, Pfeiffer is the source you can trust to make yourself and your organization more successful.

Essential Knowledge Pfeiffer produces insightful, practical, and comprehensive materials on topics that matter the most to training and HR professionals. Our Essential Knowledge resources translate the expertise of seasoned professionals into practical, how-to guidance on critical workplace issues and problems. These resources are supported by case studies, worksheets, and job aids and are frequently supplemented with CD-ROMs, websites, and other means of making the content easier to read, understand, and use.

Essential Tools Pfeiffer's Essential Tools resources save time and expense by offering proven, ready-to-use materials—including exercises, activities, games, instruments, and assessments—for use during a training or team-learning event. These resources are frequently offered in looseleaf or CD-ROM format to facilitate copying and customization of the material.

Pfeiffer also recognizes the remarkable power of new technologies in expanding the reach and effectiveness of training. While e-hype has often created whizbang solutions in search of a problem, we are dedicated to bringing convenience and enhancements to proven training solutions. All our e-tools comply with rigorous functionality standards. The most appropriate technology wrapped around essential content yields the perfect solution for today's on-the-go trainers and human resource professionals.

Pfeiffer
www.pfeiffer.com *Essential resources for training and HR professionals*

For Richard

THE **SKILLED TRAINER** SERIES

TRAINING NEEDS ASSESSMENT

METHODS, TOOLS, AND TECHNIQUES

Jean Barbazette

Pfeiffer
A Wiley Imprint
www.pfeiffer.com

Copyright © 2006 by Jean Barbazette.

Published by Pfeiffer
An Imprint of Wiley.
989 Market Street, San Francisco, CA 94103-1741 www.pfeiffer.com

Except as specifically noted below, no part of this publication may be reproduced, stored in a retrieval system, or transmitted in any form or by any means, electronic, mechanical, photocopying, recording, scanning, or otherwise, except as permitted under Section 107 or 108 of the 1976 United States Copyright Act, without either the prior written permission of the Publisher, or authorization through payment of the appropriate per-copy fee to the Copyright Clearance Center, Inc., 222 Rosewood Drive, Danvers, MA 01923, 978-750-8400, fax 978-646-8600, or on the web at www.copyright.com. Requests to the Publisher for permission should be addressed to the Permissions Department, John Wiley & Sons, Inc., 111 River Street, Hoboken, NJ 07030, phone 201-748-6011, fax 201-748-6008, or online at http://www.wiley.com/go/permissions.

Limit of Liability/Disclaimer of Warranty: While the publisher and author have used their best efforts in preparing this book, they make no representations or warranties with respect to the accuracy or completeness of the contents of this book and specifically disclaim any implied warranties of merchantability or fitness for a particular purpose. No warranty may be created or extended by sales representatives or written sales materials. The advice and strategies contained herein may not be suitable for your situation. You should consult with a professional where appropriate. Neither the publisher nor author shall be liable for any loss of profit or any other commercial damages, including but not limited to special, incidental, consequential, or other damages.

Readers should be aware that Internet websites offered as citations and/or sources for further information may have changed or disappeared between the time this was written and when it is read.

Certain pages from this book and all the materials on the accompanying CD-ROM are designed for use in a group setting and may be customized and reproduced for educational/training purposes. The reproducible pages are designated by the appearance of the following copyright notice at the foot of each page:

Training Needs Assessment. Copyright © 2006 by Jean Barbazette. Reproduced by permission of Pfeiffer, an Imprint of Wiley. www.pfeiffer.com

---

This notice may not be changed or deleted and it must appear on all reproductions as printed.

This free permission is restricted to limited customization of the CD-ROM materials for your organization and the paper reproduction of the materials for educational/training events. It does not allow for systematic or large-scale reproduction, distribution (more than 100 copies per page, per year), transmission, electronic reproduction or inclusion in any publications offered for sale or used for commercial purposes—none of which may be done without prior written permission of the Publisher.

For additional copies/bulk purchases of this book in the U.S. please contact 800-274-4434.

Pfeiffer books and products are available through most bookstores. To contact Pfeiffer directly call our Customer Care Department within the U.S. at 800-274-4434, outside the U.S. at 317-572-3985, fax 317-572-4002, or visit www.pfeiffer.com.

Pfeiffer also publishes its books in a variety of electronic formats. Some content that appears in print may not be available in electronic books.

Library of Congress Cataloging-in-Publication Data
Barbazette, Jean
    Training needs assessment : methods, tools, and techniques / Jean Barbazette.
       p. cm.
    Includes bibliographical references and index.
    ISBN-10: 0-7879-7525-7 (alk. paper)
    ISBN-13: 978-0-7879-7525-8 (alk. paper)
   1. Training needs. 2. Employees—Training of.   I. Title.
    HF5549.5.T7B288 2006
    658.3'124—dc22   2005021191

Acquiring Editor: Martin Delahoussaye
Director of Development: Kathleen Dolan Davies
Production Editor: Dawn Kilgore
Editor: Rebecca Taff
Manufacturing Supervisor: Becky Carreño
Editorial Assistant: Leota Higgins
Printed in the United States of America
Printing   10   9   8   7

CONTENTS

CONTENTS OF THE CD-ROM

Tool 1.1: Select the Right Type of Needs Analysis Chart

Tool 2.1: Performance Analysis Recommendations

Tool 2.2: Barriers Impacting Appropriate Performance

Tool 2.3: Questions to Ask About Barriers Impacting Performance

Tool 2.4: Post-Training Performance Analysis Tool

Tool 2.5: Suggested Non-Training Solutions

Tool 3.1: Fourteen Key Elements in Writing Surveys

Tool 3.2: Types of Rating Scales

Tool 4.1: Cost/Benefit Analysis Template

Tool 5.1: Sample Needs Versus Wants Survey

Tool 6.1: Goal Analysis Template

Tool 7.1: Task Analysis Observation Template

Tool 8.1: Decision Points List from Target Population Analysis

Tool 9.1: Contextual Analysis Checklist

Tool 10.1: Training Plan Template

Needs Assessor Development Plan Template

Training Planner Development Plan Template

ACKNOWLEDGMENTS

Thanks to the people who contributed to this book. Thanks to Carolyn Balling and Adrienne Kirkeby for their input and generous examples. Special thanks to Linda Ernst and Melissa Smith for timely suggestions and Kelly Barbazette for her assistance. Thanks to Eileen McDargh for her creative suggestions.

Thanks to my editors, Martin Delahoussaye, for believing in this project, and Kathleen Dolan Davies and Rebecca Taff for their valuable suggestions.

INTRODUCTION

This book is intended to help trainers and course designers who already have basic skills move their needs assessment skills to the next level. First identify the purpose of a needs assessment. Then learn how to conduct a variety of needs analysis using different data-gathering methods. Then analyze the information and develop a training plan to convince management that training is the appropriate solution. In this book, the term *needs assessment* is a general term for a three-phase process to collect information, analyze it, and create a training plan. Different types of assessments are called *needs analysis*, such as performance analysis, job/task analysis, target population analysis, etc.

Audience

This book is written for the trainer or course designer who wants to move beyond basic needs assessment skills. It is the second book in a series of six books for the intermediate trainer. The first book, *The Trainer's Journey to Competence: Tools, Assessments, and Models*, helps the trainer identify whether his or her skills are at the basic or advanced level. The resource section in this book contains the competencies to conduct needs assessments and develop a training plan. Although the main target audience is the "intermediate" trainer, new trainers with some assessment experience can benefit from the tools provided here. Training managers can use the skills in this book to develop themselves and their subordinates.

Product Description

Each chapter begins with a set of objectives and questions that are answered in that chapter. A series of models, inventories, and tools in several chapters are available to sharpen needs assessment skills. Tools and checklists are provided on the accompanying CD for easy customization and duplication. A glossary, bibliography, and index are included.

CHAPTER 1

WHAT IS NEEDS ASSESSMENT?

Chapter Objectives

- Identify why needs assessment is important
- Identify what you can do if your "client" doesn't want to spend the time and money to do an assessment
- Identify different types of needs analysis
- Identify the three phases in conducting a training needs assessment
- Learn how to set expectations and gain participation for needs assessment
- Decide who and what are assessed
- Overcome five issues when conducting needs assessment

Tools

- Select the Right Type of Needs Analysis Chart

Chapter Questions

- What is needs assessment?
- Why conduct a needs assessment?
- Why are needs assessments valuable to an organization?
- How are training needs assessments done?
- What is involved in the process of conducting a needs assessment?
- How can you convince your client to invest in a needs assessment effort?
- How can the trainer set expectations and gain participation when conducting a needs assessment?
- Who decides which people are involved and what measures are assessed?
- How are problems and barriers overcome when conducting a needs assessment?

What Is Needs Assessment?

A needs assessment is the process of collecting information about an expressed or implied organizational need that could be met by conducting training. The need can be a desire to improve current performance or to correct a deficiency. A *deficiency* is a performance that does not meet the current standard. It means that there is a prescribed or best way of doing a task and that variance from it is creating a problem. The needs assessment process helps the trainer and the person requesting training to specify the training need or performance deficiency. Assessments can be formal (using survey and interview techniques) or informal (asking some questions of those involved).

In this book, the term *needs assessment* is a general term for a three-phase process to collect information, analyze it, and create a training plan. Different types of assessments are called *needs analysis,* such as performance analysis, job/task analysis, target population analysis, and so forth. Needs assessment often involves the use of more than one type of analysis.

Why Conduct a Needs Assessment?

The purpose of a needs assessment is to answer some familiar questions: why, who, how, what, and when. Following the definitions of each type of needs assessment is the common needs analysis term.

1. *Why* conduct the training: to tie the performance deficiency to a business need and be sure the benefits of conducting the training are greater than the problems being caused by the performance deficiency. Conduct two types of analysis to answer this question: (1) *needs versus wants analysis* and (2) *feasibility analysis.*

2. *Who* is involved in the training: involve appropriate parties to solve the deficiency. Conduct a *target population analysis* to learn as much as possible about those involved in the deficiency and how to customize a training program to capture their interest.

3. *How* can the performance deficiency be fixed: training can fix the performance deficiency or suggest other remediation if training is not appropriate. Conduct a *performance analysis* to identify what skill deficiency is to be fixed by a training remedy.

4. *What* is the best way to perform: there is a better or preferred way to do a task to get the best results. Are job performance standards set by the organization, such as standard operating procedures (SOPs)? Are there governmental regulations to consider when completing the task in a required manner? Conduct a *task analysis* to identify the best way to perform.

5. *When* will training take place: the best timing to deliver training because attendance at training can be impacted by business cycles, holidays, and so forth. Conduct a *contextual analysis* to answer logistics questions.

Not all five questions must be answered as part of a needs assessment process. Later chapters will discuss how to begin a needs assessment and which types of analysis are appropriate under certain circumstances.

If trainers already know the answers to these five questions, then they know whether or not training would be appropriate. Sometimes trainers mistakenly assume that the person requesting the training has already determined the answers to these five issues and proceed to conduct training without raising these questions. A training plan that reports the conclusions from a needs assessment provides a road map that describes a business issue, problems and deficiencies that training can address, and how that will be accomplished.

Why Are Needs Assessments Valuable to an Organization?

Conducting a needs assessment protects the assets of an organization and assures that resources set aside to address training issues are conserved and used only for that purpose. A needs assessment can help determine whether training is the appropriate solution to a performance deficiency. If increasing an employee's knowledge and skills will not help resolve a deficiency, then training is not appropriate. Conducting training without assuring there is a training need is a waste of time and resources. Chapter 2 offers suggestions to correct non-training deficiencies.

How Are Training Needs Assessments Done?

A training needs assessment is a three-phase process. Decide *how* to complete each type of analysis using these three phases.

1. *Gather information:* Any analysis involves gathering information to help make appropriate decisions. Gathering information can be the process of collecting existing information or developing new information. The process can be formal or informal and involves one or more of the six types of needs analysis listed later in this chapter. Chapter 3 addresses a variety of techniques to gather information.

2. *Analyze information:* After gathering information, analyze it, interpret it, and draw conclusions from the information. It is rarely appropriate or helpful if the trainer who gathers needs analysis information *independently* analyzes and interprets information and suggests conclusions. This phase of the needs assessment is most effective as a collaborative process that includes all stakeholders. Chapters 2 and 4 through 9 discuss different types of needs analysis.

3. *Create a training plan:* After analyzing and interpreting information and offering conclusions, the information becomes the basis for a training plan which proposes how to resolve the performance deficiency. Chapter 10 describes how to develop and present a training plan.

What Is Involved in the Process of Conducting a Needs Assessment?

The process of conducting a needs assessment begins with an agreement with the client (or person requesting the training) to define the deficiency. What type of assessment information will be developed? Next, how formal or informal will the assessment process be, and who will be involved? For example, if the deficiency involves customer complaints, agree on from whom and how customer information will be gathered. Will existing customer complaints be reviewed or will a new sampling of customers be surveyed to identify the extent of the deficiency? Which employees will be interviewed or surveyed? What types of questions will be asked to develop appropriate information about the complaints or performance deficiency? What experts will be consulted to learn the best way to perform a job or task? When is the best time to conduct the training? When will assessment information be reported back to the client in a training plan or at a feedback meeting?

How to develop this information unfolds in the later chapters of this book. Tool 1.1 shows a summary of each type of analysis and what type of information develops.

Tool 1.1. Select the Right Type of Needs Analysis Chart

Type of Needs Analysis	What the Analysis Answers
Performance analysis or gap analysis	❑ Is this issue a skill deficiency? ❑ How can the deficiency be addressed? ❑ Is training the appropriate way to fix this deficiency?
Feasibility analysis	❑ Why should this training be done? ❑ Is the benefit of training greater than the cost of the current deficiency?
Needs versus wants analysis	❑ Why should this training be done? ❑ Is the deficiency tied to a business need?
Goal analysis	❑ What is the specific behavior improvement behind a vague desire?
Job/task analysis	❑ What is the best and correct way to do this task? ❑ How can this job and task be broken down into teachable parts?
Target population analysis	❑ Who is the audience for this training? ❑ What is known about them to help design and customize this training? ❑ What other populations might benefit from training?
Contextual analysis	❑ When will the training be presented? ❑ What are the other requirements to deliver the training successfully?

Training Needs Assessment. Copyright © 2006 by Jean Barbazette. Reproduced by permission of Pfeiffer, an Imprint of Wiley. www.pfeiffer.com

How Can You Convince Your Client to Invest in a Needs Assessment Effort?

Sometimes trainers are asked to conduct training without "bothering" to conduct a needs assessment. The client who requests training may be convinced that the course they request is exactly what the target population who will attend the training "needs." The client might contend that conducting a needs assessment is a waste of time and resources. It is appropriate to respect the opinions of the client. However, trainers have to trust their judgment by presenting appropriate training. This might mean asking several informal questions to identify whether the requested training is the right solution to a performance problem.

Think of conducting a needs assessment as investing a bit of time in coming up with the right solution and a greater return on the time invested. Begin by asking the person requesting the training (the client) questions about the five purposes (why, who, how, what, and when). This assures the client that the training program will be more successful when course content is customized for the specific target population. If the person you are asking doesn't know the answers to your questions, maybe this person is not the actual client and is a messenger for the client. A client is the decision maker and the person who must ultimately be pleased with the results of the training. If possible, speak directly to the client, rather than through an intermediary, who may not have the same facts and opinions as the client.

Although the client may think a needs assessment is not required, ask questions (why, who, how, what, and when) to confirm your understanding of the training request and make suggestions about how to customize and tailor the existing training and best meet the needs of the client. When you begin asking questions of the client, you are already conducting an informal needs assessment. Not asking these five types of questions before conducting training is irresponsible, since the client may end up with an inappropriate solution.

Some clients can be convinced by examples or testimonials from other clients about the importance of conducting a needs assessment. Others may agree to a needs assessment when the benefits to the bottom line are demonstrated. Drafting a quick feasibility analysis can be helpful. Chapter 4 provides information about how to conduct a feasibility analysis.

How Can the Trainer Set Expectations and Gain Participation When Conducting a Needs Assessment?

The key to setting expectations is agreeing on the above stated three-phased process with the client when identifying the performance deficiency. It is critical to agree on an outcome or objective with the client rather than agree to conduct a specific training program or event. For example, if the client asks the trainer to present a time management workshop and agrees to a bit of customizing activities in the workshop, then the client expects the trainer to deliver a slightly customized workshop. However, if the client agrees that the trainer ought to investigate ways to help his or her staff work "smarter, not harder," then different expectations have been set. Perhaps training will be a part of the solution, or perhaps not.

To gain participation from stakeholders, such as managers, supervisors, and the target population, identify the benefit for each stakeholder to participate in the needs assessment process. Also, gain the client's approval to involve each stakeholder. If approval for involving all stakeholders is not within the client's area of supervision, seek additional approval at higher levels in the organization. After identifying benefits and gaining approvals, identify each person's role and how he or she can contribute to the assessment process. Agree on a decision-making process and first assignments, and gain commitment to the next meeting.

Who Decides Which People Are Involved and What Measures Are Assessed?

The trainer who conducts the needs assessment may suggest or identify stakeholders to involve in the assessment and what measures to assess. It is usually the client who makes the decision proposed by the trainer. However, this is only one model for decision making. Different organizations have different decision-making processes. When union employees are involved, a union employee representative is also involved. Some organizations prefer a cross-functional task force to make decisions about the three phases of a needs assessment. To avoid raising additional issues or barriers, be sensitive to *who* makes decisions and to *how* decisions are made in your organization.

How Are Problems and Barriers Overcome When Conducting a Needs Assessment?

Five types of problems or barriers can arise when conducting a needs assessment. Before conducting an assessment, plan how to deal with or avoid these five issues:

1. Confidential Information

Tell those who offer information during the assessment whether the information they offer is confidential (what people say is not told to others) or anonymous (information is shared, but not who said what). Either do not ask for the name of the person completing a survey, or offer the option to provide a name. Generally, respondents are more forthcoming if they can remain anonymous. Provide an anonymous means to return the survey, perhaps in a sealed envelope, or use an electronic survey that is completed at a secure website. Consider having the results tabulated by someone outside the organization. Be sure to clarify concerns about how interview or survey information will be used.

2. Management Buy-In

Management (the client) needs to be involved during all three phases of a needs assessment (gather information, analyze information, and create a training plan). Sell the purpose and benefits of the survey or interviews to all the client's managers who are involved with the deficiency prior to collecting information. Tie the survey data to the strategic plan and/or performance review processes. Demonstrate the cost-effectiveness of gathering survey information. Anticipate management's needs and focus the survey on key work processes. Promote the purpose and benefits of the survey with supervisors and managers.

3. Unwilling Employees or Participants

Employees or customers may not be willing to spend a lot of time to complete a survey or an interview. To increase participation in information gathering, have a top executive send a cover letter with the survey or, prior to an interview, ask for the employee's cooperation in completing the survey or giving an interview. If a collective bargaining unit is involved, include their support in a cosigned cover letter with management. Get key employees to be good will ambassadors for the process. Tell the purpose of collecting the information and what will be done as a result. Sending a survey or conducting interviews sets the expectation that *something* will be done with the information. Make the distribution, the completion and return of the survey, or conducting an interview as convenient as possible. Perhaps place an article in the organization's newsletter telling the purpose of the survey or interviews and when it will be distributed.

4. Cost

During the needs assessment process, the performance deficiency usually continues. Promote the gathering of information as an investment in the progress of the organization. Do a feasibility analysis on the savings from conducting the survey or interviews versus not doing anything. Often commonly held assumptions can be validated or changed when hard data is gathered. Use existing data regarding the deficiency to avoid the cost of asking for what is already available.

5. Interrupts Work

Time is money. Taking employees away from productive work to complete a survey or an interview may detract from job results. Keep the survey brief, streamlined, and attractive in appearance. Insert the survey in the employee's paycheck or have completion coincide with the first day of another event. When conducting interviews, write out key questions prior to the interview. Set specific appointments with a starting and ending time. Depending on the complexity of the performance issues, most one-on-one interviews beyond 30 to 60 minutes usually fail to gather significant information.

After planning to address each of the five barriers and understanding the three phases of needs assessment, you are ready to identify different techniques to gather information.

The case study that follows will help illustrate how to deal with several issues about needs assessment addressed in this chapter.

CASE STUDY: IS THIS A SWEET DEAL?[1]

Directions: Review the situation below and identify what information Pete ought to develop through a needs assessment before presenting the Vice President with a cost-effective solution to their personnel issues. What types of analysis would you suggest he conduct?

---

[1]Used with permission from *Instant Case Studies* by Jean Barbazette, © 2004, Pfeiffer, pages 247–249.

Pete is the training coordinator at Sweet Life Inc., a fast-growing chain of retail candy shops. The shops are located in large malls and offer a variety of "home made" type sweets. Each shop has at least four people on shift during store hours. There is a manager and three staff people who cook, clean, and sell.

The vice president of store operations is concerned about the quality of store personnel, who are recruited, interviewed, oriented, and trained in the variety of demanding tasks. All of these tasks and more fall on the already burdened shoulders of the store manager. After several discussions with the VP of store operations, Pete's first thought is to improve the interviewing skills of store managers. This type of training would help improve the quality of store personnel hired by the store managers. Pete has the VP's approval to work toward a solution, but keep the cost down.

1. What is the purpose or objective of conducting a needs assessment?

2. What type of information does Pete need to develop before proceeding with interviewing skills training? What types of analysis should he conduct?

3. Who should be involved in the assessment?

Possible Case Answers

1. The purpose of the needs assessment is to identify how to improve the quality of store personnel that are recruited, interviewed, oriented, and trained.

2. What type of information does Pete need to develop and ask before proceeding with interviewing skills training?

   - What are the vice president's concerns about the quality of store personnel? (*Use a task analysis and target population analysis.*)

   - What are the current recruitment and hiring practices and what is the cause of quality deficiencies? (*Conduct a performance analysis.*)

- To what extent are store managers burdened and how does this affect the recruitment, hiring, orienting, and training of new employees? (*Conduct a job analysis.*)

- How would skills training in interviewing improve the situation? (*Conduct a task analysis and feasibility analysis.*)

- Is the suspected lack of skills to recruit, hire, orient, and train employees a widespread deficiency for all store managers? (*Conduct a target population analysis.*)

2. Who should be involved in the assessment?

   - VP of operations

   - Store managers from a variety of stores

Not every type of needs analysis is used in this situation. This case study will appear in later chapters to help explain the application of different types of needs analysis. The next chapter discusses performance analysis and why this type of analysis is usually completed before other types of analysis.

CHAPTER 2

IS IT A TRAINING NEED?

How to Conduct a Performance Analysis

Chapter Objectives

- Identify how to conduct a performance analysis
- Use informal methods for performance analysis
- Use formal methods for performance analysis
- Discuss Issues and concerns about performance analysis

Tools

- Performance Analysis Recommendations
- Barriers Impacting Appropriate Performance
- Questions to Ask About Barriers Impacting Performance
- Post-Training Performance Analysis
- Suggested Non-Training Solutions

Chapter Questions

- What is performance analysis?
- What is the purpose of performance analysis?
- How is performance analysis conducted?
- What is post-training performance analysis?
- What are the problems and cautions when conducting performance analysis?
- What needs to be done with the information collected?

What Is Performance Analysis?

Performance analysis is also known as "gap" analysis. Performance analysis looks at an employee's current performance and identifies whether or not an employee is performing as desired. This analysis presumes there is an implied or explicit standard for current performance. The more explicit the standard for current performance, the easier it will be to describe the "gap" or performance deficiency. In their book *Training for Impact*, Dana Gaines Robinson and James C. Robinson[1] encourage trainers to get the person who is requesting training to describe the deficiency using a series of "is" and "should" questions. For example, what *is* the employee doing that is incorrect? What *should* the employee be doing instead?

If the employee is not performing as desired, identify what the employee is doing incorrectly. Next, Robert Mager and Peter Pipe[2] suggest you identify whether this deficiency is important enough to do anything about. If the deficiency is not important, move on to other issues. Finally, ask why the employee does the task in a deficient manner. A *deficiency is a difference with a negative connotation,* implying that the employee is not meeting a known standard for performance. Identify whether the deficiency is caused by lack of knowledge or skills or whether other issues are getting in the way of performing to the standard. For example, in the case study from Chapter 1, Pete suspects that store managers might be overwhelmed by the pace of business and the pressure to get employees recruited, hired, oriented, and trained as quickly as possible.

It may be appropriate to discuss the deficient performance with the employees as well as the supervisors and those who receive the work product from the deficient performance to clearly understand all aspects of the deficiency.

What Is the Purpose of Performance Analysis?

The purpose of conducting a performance analysis is to identify the cause of deficient performance so appropriate corrective action can occur. More specifically, is the issue or problem caused by a skill deficiency? If so, then a training

---

[1]Robinson, Dana Gaines, and Robinson, James C. *Training for Impact: How to Link Training to Business Needs and Measure the Results.* San Francisco: Jossey-Bass, 1989.

[2]Mager, R.F., and Pipe, Peter. *Analyzing Performance Problems: Or You Really Oughta Wanna.* Atlanta, GA: Center for Effective Performance, 1997.

solution would be appropriate. If the issue or problem is not a skill deficiency, then a non-training solution is more appropriate. For example, if an employee knows how to do a task correctly and chooses not to do the task, no amount of training will get the employee to perform as desired. Look at the reason the employee chooses not to do the task correctly and determine whether there are obstacles, no sanctions, no feedback, or other causes of not performing appropriately. Non-training solutions might include removing obstacles, providing sanctions, and feedback.

It is appropriate to conduct a performance analysis before any other type of needs assessment since the issue may not require a training solution. Most other forms of needs assessment involve developing information about the task and the target population. If training is not an appropriate solution, conducting a performance analysis first will save time and resources.

How Is Performance Analysis Conducted?

Whenever a request is made to conduct a training program, ask the client requesting the training what the training is intended to accomplish. It is critical that the trainer agree to help the client reach an outcome, rather than agree to conduct a training event. Three types of performance analysis can be used to identify whether conducting training will help the client reach the training objective. The first two methods are informal and the third is more structured.

"Oh, So" Performance Analysis Method

When asked to conduct training, begin to conduct a performance analysis with a few informal questions of the requestor using the "oh, so" method. This informal assessment conversation might sound something like this:

Manager: "I'd like you to conduct a time management workshop for my department."

Trainer: "*Oh*, tell me more about that."

Manager: "Okay, I'd like the training to be held next week for my group."

Trainer: "*So*, if we conduct a time management workshop for your department next week, what do you hope to accomplish?"

Manager: "I want everyone in our department to work smarter, not harder."

Trainer: "*Oh,* I see. *So* what does working smarter look like?"

Manager: "Well, everyone would be more organized in approaching his or her work."

Trainer: "Are your employees disorganized?"

Manager: "Maybe. I'm not sure if everyone is disorganized. There's a lot of duplicate work going on."

Trainer: "*So* you would like the time management training to eliminate duplicate work?"

Manager: "Exactly."

Trainer: "*So,* what's causing duplicate work to occur? Give me an example of how this occurred recently."

From this brief conversation, the trainer has led the manager through a series of questions to identify duplicate work that might be corrected by conducting a time management workshop. Duplicate work might also be eliminated by more supervisory oversight or by improving the method of assigning work. Further information must be developed to reach learning objectives that are yet to be agreed on.

Can-Can't/Will-Won't Performance Analysis Method

Can-can't/will-won't is a second informal method of conducting a performance analysis. Use the simple four-cell matrix in Tool 2.1 to identify whether the employee's deficient performance is caused by lack of skill, an unwilling attitude, lack of appropriate resources, not enough time, or other issues hindering completion of the task. The horizontal axis asks whether the employee can or can't perform as desired. The vertical axis asks whether the employee is willing or unwilling to perform the task to the desired standard. The four cells suggest a remedy for each combination of the four circumstances.

For example, in Cell 1, if an employee can perform as desired, is willing to perform the task, and is not performing as desired, continue to look for another obstacle to doing the task. The employee needs to be supported with time and resources. In Cell 2, if the employee can't do the task and is willing to do it, then

Tool 2.1. Performance Analysis Recommendations

	Can Do It	Can't Do It
Willing to Do It	1. Can/will situation • Look for another cause for deficient performance • Support with time and resources • Provide coaching	2. Can't/will situation • Provide skills training • Conduct on-the-job training • Could be lack of resources, equipment, tools, etc. • Look for another cause
Won't Do It	3. Can/won't situation • Discuss poor attitude • Identify consequences • Provide feedback • Provide coaching • Supervise practice	4. Can't/won't situation • Provide skills training • Supervise practice • Discuss poor attitude • Identify benefits • Investigate possible other problem

© 1995 Carolyn Balling and Jean Barbazette. All rights reserved. Reprinted with permission.

some type of skills training might be useful. The training can be formal classroom training, on-the-job training, or informal coaching. In Cell 3, if the employee can do the task and is unwilling to do the task, no amount of training will be useful. Look for remedies that include other strategies, such as a counseling session to discuss the employee's poor attitudes. Help the employee understand the consequences of poor performance, such as no pay raises or job promotion. If the employee receives no feedback (positive or negative), how can the employee be encouraged to perform as desired? Coaching the employee and supervising the employee more closely are additional strategies for this situation. In Cell 4, if the employee can't do the task and is unwilling to do the task, the situation may call for further investigation to sort out the training and non-training issues. Skills training is probably needed, along with supervised practice and a discussion with the employee about the benefits of performing as desired. A list of non-training solutions is provided at the end of this chapter.

The case study below will illustrate what type of questions can be asked when identifying the cause of deficient performance using the "can/can't-will/won't" matrix.

PERFORMANCE ANALYSIS CASE STUDY

Directions: As you read the following case study, identify the answers to these two questions:

1. Who would you want to interview besides the director of public relations and fund raising?

2. What questions would you ask to uncover all dimensions of the real problem?

The director of public relations and fund raising at Community Medical Center has asked you to present a "Guest Relations Workshop" for all employees who have patient contact.

The director has described the Emergency Room employees as a particularly "needy" group for this type of training. He suggests their lack of normal social graces and a few cases of burnout are giving the Medical Center a bad reputation and making it difficult to raise funds in the community.

Just last week, Mrs. Wealthy Donor, a significant benefactor for the Medical Center, was made to wait several hours for treatment of a minor but painful injury. The wait was quite uncomfortable, and she was all but forgotten by the insensitive staff.

Possible Case Answers

1. Interviewing the Emergency Room supervisor as well as Emergency Room employees would be appropriate. Interviewing Mrs. Wealthy Donor might produce additional pertinent information, but talking with her would be at the discretion of the director of public relations and fund raising.

2. Questions for the director and other employees working in the emergency room include questions that seek information about *skill deficiency (can/can't):*

   • What type of information was given to the patient?

   • What are past indicators of satisfactory or unsatisfactory performance in the Emergency Room?

   • What kind of complaints do you hear from patients with minor injuries?

   • What is the intake process in the Emergency Room? Was that process followed when Mrs. Wealthy Donor was there?

   Questions that seek information about the *employee's attitude (will/won't):*

   • What are Emergency Room employees doing that demonstrates that patient relations training is needed?

   • What do department reports tell you about what you expect Emergency Room employees to do that they are not doing?

Sometimes the answers to these questions will indicate that the situation is more complex than first anticipated and that more information is needed to make an appropriate decision about what training or other intervention is appropriate. Here are some questions that indicate a more formal performance analysis is needed:

- How typical was the wait experienced by Mrs. Wealthy Donor in the Emergency Room on that evening?

- To what extent is this incident counter to current satisfaction trends given in weekly reports?

- What other activity occurred in the Emergency Room on that evening that impacted levels of service and waiting time?

Formal Performance Analysis Tools

The last three questions above from the can-can't/will-won't informal performance analysis indicate that a more formal approach to performance analysis is needed to get to the cause of the problem. Formal performance analysis uses a tool or a chart to ask a series of questions in an organized manner and focuses on nine separate dimensions. The following performance analysis tool organizes questions in a nine-cell matrix showing three basic types of barriers to performing as desired: physical, emotional, and intellectual. These three types of barriers can occur on three levels: personal, environmental, and informational. Tool 2.2 shows the types of barriers to performance. Questions to ask about each barrier impacting appropriate performance follow the chart, in Tool 2.3.

Before summarizing how to conduct a performance analysis and what to do with the information, there is one more type of performance analysis to be considered, post-training performance analysis.

What Is Post-Training Performance Analysis?

Post-training performance analysis occurs after training has been completed. It usually occurs when the supervisor of an employee who attended a training session is not pleased with the results. The supervisor may ask the trainer, "Why didn't the employee learn to do anything?" Tool 2.4 can help identify why the employee who completed training cannot do the task the class meant to teach.

Tool 2.2. Barriers Impacting Appropriate Performance

	Physical	Emotional	Intellectual
	Capacity	Motives	Skill/Knowledge

Personal	❑ Lack of strength
	❑ Lack of dexterity
	❑ Lack of stamina
	❑ Lack of attentiveness
	❑ Lack of concentration
	❑ Inability to learn
	  new tasks
		❑ Lack of internalized
		  reward system
		❑ Lack of personal goals
		❑ Lack of initiative
		❑ Personal values
		  inconsistent with
		  mission
			❑ Lack of basic skills
			❑ Lack of specific
			  task-related skills
			❑ Lack of knowledge
			  of policy/procedures
			  procedures
			❑ Lacks understanding
			  of supportive
			  knowledge

	Resources	Incentives	Procedures or Methods

Environment	❑ Inadequate personnel
	❑ Inadequate raw
	  materials
	❑ Inadequate supplies
	❑ Inadequate equipment
	❑ Inadequate space
	❑ Inadequate support
	  services
	❑ Inadequate energy
		❑ Good performance
		  is not positively
		  reinforced
		❑ Poor performance
		  is positively reinforced
		❑ Poor performance is
		  not linked to negative
		  consequences
			❑ Dated materials
			❑ Unreasonable
			  deadlines
			❑ Unclear chain of
			  command
			❑ Unclear reporting
			  structure
			❑ Lack of access to
			  decision process
			❑ Work not oriented
			  to performers
			❑ Extensive paperwork/
			  red tape

	Task Expectations	Mission	Information Flow

Information	❑ Inconsistent task
	  requirements
	❑ Conflicting time
	  demands
	❑ Inadequate task
	  assignment
	❑ Unnecessarily
	  complex tasks
	❑ Duplicative task
	  assignments
	❑ Infrequently used
	  tasks
		❑ No policy
		❑ Conflicting policies
		❑ Changing policies
		❑ Conflicting
		  assignments
		❑ Task goals
		  inconsistent with
		  organization's
		  mission
			❑ Changing
			  information
			❑ Lack of information
			❑ Lack of accurate
			  data
			❑ Lack of timely data
			❑ Lack of complete
			  data
			❑ Lack of feedback
			❑ Lack of monitoring

© 1983 *Instructional Systems Design*, by Robert Carkhuff and Sharon Fisher. Amherst, MA: HRD Press. All rights reserved. Used with permission of the publisher.

Tool 2.3. Questions to Ask About Barriers Impacting Performance

Use these questions do learn more about what type of barrier might be impacting an employee's performance:

Personal Barriers

Physical/Capacity

- Does the individual lack the strength, dexterity, or stamina to do the task?
- Does the individual lack attentiveness or concentration to do the task?
- Does the individual have the ability to learn new tasks?

Emotional/Motives

- Does the individual set personal goals and have internal rewards for success?
- Does the individual lack initiative to do the task?
- Do the individual's personal values conflict with task accomplishment?

Intellectual/Skill and Knowledge

- Does the individual lack basic or task-related skills?
- Does the individual know how policies and procedures impact doing this task?
- Does the individual have an understanding of supportive knowledge to do this task?

Training Needs Assessment. Copyright © 2006 by Jean Barbazette. Reproduced by permission of Pfeiffer, an Imprint of Wiley. www.pfeiffer.com

Tool 2.3. Questions to Ask About Barriers Impacting Performance, Cont'd

Environmental Barriers

Physical/Resources

- Are adequate personnel available to do the task?
- Are adequate raw materials, supplies, equipment, and energy available to do the task?
- Are adequate space and support services available to do the task?

Emotional/Incentives

- Is good performance of the task positively reinforced?
- Is poor performance positively reinforced?
- Are there negative consequences for poor performance?

Intellectual/Procedures or Methods

- Are materials to perform the task out-of-date?
- Are deadlines for task completion reasonable?
- Is the chain of command over the task and the reporting structure clear?
- Is the work oriented to the performers?
- Is paperwork or red tape extensive and creates a barrier to task performance?

Training Needs Assessment. Copyright © 2006 by Jean Barbazette. Reproduced by permission of Pfeiffer, an Imprint of Wiley. www.pfeiffer.com

Tool 2.3. Questions to Ask About Barriers Impacting Performance, Cont'd

Information Barriers

Physical/Task Expectations

- Are task requirements consistent?
- Are there conflicting time demands for individuals performing the task?
- Are tasks assigned adequately?
- Are tasks unnecessarily complex?
- Are duplicate assignments made for the same task?
- How frequently are tasks done?

Emotional/Mission

- Does a policy exist governing how the task is done?
- Are there conflicting policies for how the task is done?
- How often is the policy changed?
- Are individuals given conflicting assignments?
- Is the task goal consistent with the organization's mission?

Information/Information Flow

- How frequently does information change?
- Does the individual have enough accurate, timely, and complete information to do the task?
- How does the individual get feedback when the task is done incorrectly?
- How is the individual and task completion monitored or supervised?

Training Needs Assessment. Copyright © 2006 by Jean Barbazette. Reproduced by permission of Pfeiffer, an Imprint of Wiley. www.pfeiffer.com

Tool 2.4. Post-Training Performance Analysis

Ask questions 1, 2, and 3 of the instructor and/or the learner about what happened during training by placing a checkmark in the blanks that describes the learner's behavior.

1. Describe the learner's level of participation during training:

    _____ Did not attend the entire course

    _____ Was not involved mentally or physically

    _____ Paid attention, listened, and observed others

    _____ Evaluated, analyzed, and questioned during class

    _____ Set personal objectives based on course content

    _____ Participated appropriately so personal and course objectives were met

2. Describe the degree to which the learner's individual and course objectives were met at the end of training:

    _____ Did not meet all objectives

    _____ Has factual understanding of course content

    _____ Can interpret cause-and-effect relationships of content

    _____ Can interpret implications from facts and concepts presented in content

    _____ Can perform different steps of the skills presented

3. Describe how completely the learned skill was performed in the classroom (or simulated if on-the-job training was done):

    _____ Used appropriate resources: people, tools, and materials

    _____ Partially performed the skill

    _____ Performed the skill correctly

    _____ Performed the skill correctly under the prescribed conditions

Training Needs Assessment. Copyright © 2006 by Jean Barbazette. Reproduced by permission of Pfeiffer, an Imprint of Wiley. www.pfeiffer.com

Tool 2.4. Post-Training Performance Analysis, Cont'd

_____ Performed the skill correctly under the prescribed conditions, meeting all standards

_____ Can perform the entire skill to the minimum level of achievement

_____ Can perform the entire skill above the level of achievement

Ask questions 4 and 5 of the learner and the supervisor.

4. Identify how well the learner applied or transferred the newly learned skill on the job:

   Appropriate resources (people, tools, and materials) are:

   _____ Not always used *(transfer incomplete)*

   _____ Always used *(transfer complete)*

   Prescribed method, procedures, or process is:

   _____ Not always used *(transfer incomplete)*

   _____ Always used *(transfer complete)*

   Prescribed conditions are a barrier to performance:

   _____ Always *(transfer incomplete)*

   _____ Sometimes *(transfer incomplete)*

   _____ Never *(transfer complete)*

   Skill performance standards are:

   _____ Not always met *(transfer incomplete)*

   _____ Always met *(transfer complete)*

5. To what extent does the learner get results using the prescribed performance designed to meet minimum standards?

   _____ Results *do not meet* minimum standards

   _____ Results *just meet* minimum standards

   _____ Results *exceed* minimum standards

Training Needs Assessment. Copyright © 2006 by Jean Barbazette. Reproduced by permission of Pfeiffer, an Imprint of Wiley. www.pfeiffer.com

Once the cause of deficient performance is determined, you may not need to proceed further through the survey. Questions 1, 2, and 3 concern what occurred during the training and can be asked of the instructor or the learner. Questions 4 and 5 ask what occurred when the employee returned to work following the training and can be asked of the learner and the supervisor. Here's a case study sample using Tool 2.4.

POST-TRAINING PERFORMANCE ANALYSIS CASE STUDY

We continue with the case study introduced in Chapter 1 about Pete's Sweet Life, Inc., candy stores. Suppose that interview training was conducted to help the store managers make a better hiring decision and the vice president of store operations challenges Pete about the results. Read the next installment in this case study, and see how Post-Training Performance Analysis can be used to ask questions of the trainers who taught the two sessions of this class to the store managers.

The vice president of store operations tells Pete that Alex, one of the store managers who attended the training, has not retained "anything" that was taught in the class and perhaps he ought to attend the class again. The VP says turnover at Alex's store is higher than at the stores of the other managers who have attended this training. Alex seems stressed and overwhelmed by the day-to-day activity at the store. Alex told the VP that the interviewing methods taught in the class are not practical for the types of candidates he interviews. The class was "a waste of time."

Tool 2.4. Post-Training Performance Analysis

Case study questions about Alex's level of participation in the selection interviewing training:

   a. Did Alex attend the entire eight hours of the workshop?

   b. To what extent did Alex participate in the discussions, role plays, and question exercises?

   c. To what extent did Alex pay attention and listen to others in the class?

d. Did Alex write selected individual objectives in his hand-out material?

e. What questions did Alex ask during class?

2. Case study questions about the degree to which Alex's personal and course objectives were met:

a. Based on the test given at the end of the workshop, did Alex meet the course objectives?

b. Did Alex score high enough on the test at the end of the workshop to demonstrate a factual understanding of the course material?

c. How did Alex answer the questions in the hiring case study discussion that demonstrates his understanding of interview questions and their relationship to predicting a successful job candidate?

d. To what extent did Alex discuss his understanding of how to review a job application?

e. Describe how Alex performed during the five steps of the role play interview.

3. Case study questions about how interviewing skills were performed by Alex:

a. Did Alex use the question worksheet, sample job application to write appropriate questions of a job candidate?

b. Did Alex perform all or part of the interview skills; if only parts, which parts?

c. To what extent did Alex ask appropriate questions of the job candidate?

d. Was Alex able to ask all of the questions within the fifteen-minute role play?

e. Were all of the questions appropriately phrased?

f. Did Alex perform the entire job candidate interview so that he met or exceeded the requirements?

4. In the case study, Alex and his regional manager would be asked these questions:

   a. How often were company job applications and job aid with interview questions used to interview actual job candidates?

      ☐ not always   ☐ always

   b. Did Alex use the five-step process to interview job candidates?

      ☐ not always   ☐ always

   c. Were the conditions in the learning objectives (use the job aid, interview the candidate without assistance from another employee, ask appropriate follow-up questions) a barrier to conducting the job interview?

      ☐ always   ☐ sometimes   ☐ never

   d. Was Alex able to complete the five steps in the interview process and ask appropriate question?

      ☐ not always   ☐ always

5. In the case study, Alex and his regional manager would be asked the following questions. The results from using appropriate interviewing skills would be hiring the right job candidate and having that person stay with the store for a reasonable period of time.

   a. In order to hire the right employee, was Alex able to recruit, hire, orient, and train the new employees in the two weeks it typically takes other managers to do this task?

   b. Did the new employee remain on the job at least six months before leaving for a new job?

   c. Did the new employee succeed and was promoted to the next level (shift lead person) at the store?

Once these questions have been answered, it is possible for the VP of operations, along with Alex and Pete, to decide whether Alex really did learn the five-step interviewing process during the class and whether or not he needs to attend training again. There also appear to be additional factors that impact Alex's ability to use the interview process successfully on the job.

Two final issues remain concerning performance analysis.

What Are the Problems and Cautions When Conducting Performance Analysis?

When conducting performance analysis, the trainer can run into problems or barriers. One problem can be the potential client who wants the trainer to put on a training event without wasting time doing any analysis. This issue was addressed in Chapter 1 by suggesting that the trainer begin asking questions to clarify what the training is to accomplish and how the content can be customized to meet the client's needs. Often time is saved and resources are preserved through an assessment.

Another problem could be access to people who have information about past and desired performance. Work with the client or the trainer's manager to gain access to those with information about performance issues. It is understandable that management might not want to involve external customers in an analysis process. Sometimes customer survey information or business statistics can reveal desired information.

Additional problems that can arise when doing a needs assessment are addressed in Chapter 3.

What Needs to Be Done with the Information Collected?

Information developed through performance analysis interviews and surveys is best reported anonymously. Be sure those who answer interview and survey questions know that the information they provide will be kept anonymous, and that the information is NOT confidential.

The information collected in a performance analysis can help the client decide whether or not training will make a difference in the employee's performance. The information collected from the answers to the questions posed in the four tools so far in this chapter is sorted into two categories: skill deficiency (training is the appropriate solution) and attitude or other barriers (training is not appropriate). Performance analysis information can help cost justify training by saving the organization time and money and to avoid applying a training solution where there is no skill deficiency. Non-training solutions suggested in this chapter include removing barriers, providing coaching, creating job aids, giving supervisory support, sharing consequences, providing feedback, and supervising employee practice sessions until a skill is fully developed. Tool 2.5 shows a variety of non-training solutions using the framework introduced in Tool 2.2.

Various methods to make recommendations and report information are discussed in Chapter 10. The next chapter discusses several techniques to gather information.

Tool 2.5. Suggested Non-Training Solutions

	Physical	Emotional	Intellectual
	Capacity	Motives	Skill/Knowledge
Personal	Make the task less challenging by creating lighter units Have more frequent breaks Screen job candidates for required physical skills	Create or revise a reward system Help workers set personal goals Reward initiative	Demonstration of procedures Practice following a demonstration Review of policy/ procedures Read or review supportive knowledge Provide a job aid Coach inconsistent performance
	Resources	Incentives	Procedures or Methods
Environment	Hire additional personnel Buy more raw materials Buy more supplies Buy more equipment Expand space Outsource support services Increase energy	Positively reinforce good performance Reprimand poor performance Link poor performance to negative consequences	Update materials Set reasonable deadlines Clarify chain of command Clarify reporting structure Provide access to decision process Orient work to performers Streamline paperwork
	Task Expectations	Mission	Information Flow
Information	Make task requirements consistent Eliminate conflicting time demands Clarify task assignment Simplify complex tasks Eliminate duplicate task assignments Increase frequency of tasks	Create or clarify a policy Resolve conflicting policies Stabilize existing policies Resolve conflicting assignments Make task goals consistent with organization's mission	Update information Provide more information Share accurate data Provide timely data Provide complete data Provide feedback Monitoring work

Training Needs Assessment. Copyright © 2006 by Jean Barbazette. Reproduced by permission of Pfeiffer, an Imprint of Wiley. www.pfeiffer.com

CHAPTER 3

HOW TO GATHER INFORMATION

Chapter Objectives

- Use informal methods and using existing information
- Learn how to construct a survey
- Define statistical significance
- Use interviewing techniques

Tools

- Fourteen Key Elements in Writing Surveys
- Types of Rating Scales

Chapter Questions

- What is the purpose or objective of collecting the information?
- Where can you find existing information, or does new information have to be gathered?

- What is the difference between informal and formal information collection?
- What are the key elements in constructing written surveys?
- What are different forms for survey questions?
- What are guidelines to collect statistically significant information?
- When and why are interviews appropriate to gather information?

What Is the Purpose or Objective of Collecting the Information?

Gather information is the first phase of a three-phase needs assessment process. Any assessment involves gathering information to help make appropriate decisions. Information can validate or dispel assumptions. Uninformed decisions are dangerous to the health of an organization. As stated in Chapter 1, there are seven different types of needs analysis, and each has a specific purpose or objective. After discussing the objective of an assessment with the client, write a purpose statement or analysis objective that summarizes what the client and the needs assessor agree upon. For example, *"Given the request for time management training for executives and administrative assistants, we will collect information from these teams of two to identify time wasters along with their suggestions about what would help these teams work 'smarter, not harder.'"* Notice that this objective does not promise that a training session will be offered as the solution to assumed time management issues.

Where Can You Find Existing Information, or Does New Information Have to Be Gathered?

It is usually easier and less costly to gather existing information than to gather new information. Look in several places for existing information, such as:

- Operations and productivity statistics and reports
- Prior surveys or interview information
- Financial records
- Purchase order and inventory reports
- Organization databases
- Logs or records of employee activities and hours
- Personnel records or performance review information
- Customer satisfaction information reports
- Complaints or grievances
- Print media
- Information on the organization's website
- Materials from previous training programs attended by a specific group

Be aware that certain information in personnel records, including performance review information, may be confidential and not open to review. This type of information can only be used for its original purpose.

Often existing information can provide either the exact information to clarify assumptions or describe the extent of an issue—or information that can become the basis for further discovery. Continuing with the example above about requested time management training, perhaps the communication tools used by teams of two can be reviewed. Information about the frequency of meetings between the teams of two can also help reveal productivity issues and possible time wasters. Notice that the assessment objective addresses performance issues, and the type of analysis called for in the objective is a *performance analysis*.

What Is the Difference Between Informal and Formal Information Collection?

Typically, informal information collection is done verbally through a conversation, and perhaps a few written notes are recorded. Formal information collection involves the use of written surveys, interviews of stakeholders, and other structured methods of collecting information. If a formal collection method is needed, consider the key elements from Tool 3.1 and described below when constructing a written survey.

Tool 3.1. Fourteen Key Elements in Writing Surveys

Use this checklist and list of questions when developing written surveys:

1. Write your *objective* for the assessment.

2. Decide what will be done with the *results* of the assessment.

3. Decide *who* will interpret the data, report data, and so forth.

Training Needs Assessment. Copyright © 2006 by Jean Barbazette. Reproduced by permission of Pfeiffer, an Imprint of Wiley. www.pfeiffer.com

Tool 3.1. Fourteen Key Elements in Writing Surveys, Cont'd

4. Decide *who* you will survey (level or levels of employees, customers, etc.)

5. Gather *preliminary information*

6. Identify *issues* to assess and *sequence* issues.

7. Decide the *focus* of the assessment.
   - Skill test
   - Attitude survey, values clarification
   - Problem identification
   - Preference, interest, opinion
   - Self-perception, perception of others

8. Decide on question *format* that ensures ease of answering the survey
   - Multiple choice
   - Continuum
   - Rating
   - Ranking

9. Write clear and simple *instructions* for completing the survey.

10. *Write* and *sequence* questions.

11. Check the *reliability* of a questionnaire by administering it at different times under the same conditions. If you obtain the same results from multiple administrations, the questions are reliable.

12. Check *validity* of the content. Do your questions measure conditions that meet the objectives of the assessment?

13. Write a *cover letter* from an executive.

14. In *scoring*, look for *trends and patterns* in behavior, attitudes, or values. *Exact* measures and percentages are rarely meaningful.

Training Needs Assessment. Copyright © 2006 by Jean Barbazette. Reproduced by permission of Pfeiffer, an Imprint of Wiley. www.pfeiffer.com

What Are the Key Elements in Constructing Written Surveys?

Using the request for time management training for teams of two as the example, here are ways the fourteen key elements in Tool 3.1 can be used in constructing a survey. Each element is defined below, and the filled-in example is written in *italics*. This example is based on an actual survey used to assess the direction of teams of two in a specific organization.

1. Write your *objective* for the assessment: for example, *given the request for time management training for executives and administrative assistants, we will collect information from these teams of two to identify time wasters along with their suggestions about what would help these teams work "smarter, not harder."*

2. Decide what will be done with the *results* of the assessment: for example, *the results will be tabulated and presented to management and administrative assistant teams to decide what type of training, if any, will be presented along with other recommendations.*

3. Decide *who* will interpret the data: for example, *the consultant's team will report the data to a task force of three teams of two. Conclusions and recommendations will be drawn by that group.*

4. Decide *who* you will survey (level or levels of employees, customers, and so forth): for example, *all candidates at the executive and senior manager levels and their administrative assistants will receive the survey. This represented 120 people in the actual example.*

5. Gather *preliminary information*: for example, *the organization's task force reviewed three versions of the survey and suggested different dimensions to include in the survey.*

6. Identify *issues* to assess and *sequence* issues: for example, *twenty issues were assessed by mutual agreement of the task force and the consultant. The issues were randomly sequenced to avoid a pattern of answers. Sometimes like items are sequenced together to help the participant respond to different themes.*

7. Decide the *focus of assessment*: for example, *the survey is self-perception for the administrative assistants, and perception of others when completed by the managers.* Other surveys might include the opinions of peers or customers.

TOOL: what it can do

8. Decide on the question *format* that ensures ease of answering the ___ for example, *a rating scale is given.* Other options could include "agree" and "disagree" choices on a continuum. Formats that ask how frequently a person performs a task make self-reports of knowledge and skills a bit more accurate.

9. Make *instructions* for completing the survey clear and simple: for example, *see the survey* [Figures 3.1 and 3.2] *and cover letter* [Figure 3.4] *for sample instructions. The survey was sent as an email attachment and printed, then returned by mail, fax, or email attachment, depending on the level of anonymity sought by the person completing the survey.* Include the length of time to return the survey. When surveys are posted on the organization's intranet, inform the survey participants how long the survey will be available for completion.

10. *Write* and *sequence* questions: [See the survey for the questions and sequence.] Additional information is also available later in the chapter about writing different types of questions. When deciding how many questions to ask, identify the level of interest the respondents have in this topic. Surveys longer than one page tend to test the patience of most survey respondents.

11. Check the *reliability* of the questionnaire by administering it at different times under the same conditions. If you obtain the same results, the questions are reliable: *No reliability test was done for this sample assessment.*

12. Check *validity* of the content. Do your questions measure conditions that meet the objectives of the assessment? For example, *the questions did meet the objectives of the assessment since information was developed about the team of two issues.*

13. Write a *cover letter* from an executive. [See Figure 3.4.]

14. In *scoring,* look for *trends and patterns* in behavior, attitudes, or values. *Exact* measures and percentages are rarely meaningful, even with large numbers of participants return a survey. [See sample scores and trends in Figure 3.3.]

A summary form of the key elements for writing surveys follows.

What Are Different Forms for Survey Questions?

When writing survey questions, consider using one of five types of questions. Knowing the purpose of each form of question can help you collect the appropriate information to meet the objective of the survey. Surveys that contain only one type of question avoid confusing the survey reader.

Multiple Choice

The purpose of a multiple choice question is often to test knowledge, skill perception, reasoning, or opinions or when more than one option could apply. For example, if survey recipients are managers who might be candidates for selection interview training, assessing their knowledge of appropriate interviewing techniques can identify training needs. For example:

Which are legally permissible questions to ask of a candidate for employment:

   a. Who was your previous employer?
   b. What child care arrangements do you have?
   c. How old are you?
   d. How will you get to work?

[handwritten margin note: "Is How much TIME can we have them?"]

True/False or Two-Alternative Response

The purpose of asking a two-alternative question is often to measure cause to effect, or effect to cause. The two alternatives can be true or false, yes or no, agree or disagree, or other options. Be careful to ask about a single issue, unless a combination of two issues is part of the question. For example:

True or false: All offers for employment must follow negative results of a drug test and a reference check.

Two negative results must be present to make this a true statement.

[handwritten: ANY OPPTY TO ASK THEIR BOSSES? THEY HIRED THEM, RIGHT?]

Rating Scale

The purpose of a rating scale is to identify knowledge, intensity of opinions, or values held by the survey respondents. For example:

> On a scale of 1 to 10 (10 = best), *rate* the following as predictors of job success:
>
> _____ length of service on previous jobs
>
> _____ no employment gaps on an application
>
> _____ similar or increased salary in new job
>
> _____ attendance record
>
> _____ amount of vacation previously taken

[handwritten: 20K - 10K - 1K / 19K; 1st 19K/2 = 9.5; 10K-1=9K]

Another example from Figure 3.1 would be to ask the manager to rate the administrative assistant on twenty tasks. Each task is rated two times using two scales. Here are the scales:

Column A Rating:
Current Behavior

4 = definitely does this

3 = somewhat does this

2 = rarely does this

1 = does not do this

Column B Rating:
Future Behavior

4 = strongly encourage my assistant to do this

3 = slightly encourage

2 = slightly discourage my assistant

1 = strongly discourage my assistant

Another format for a rating question is to use a semantic differential scale to assess the reaction or intensity of the survey respondent's opinions. For example:

> Circle an appropriate number to rate the following as an important characteristic in a job candidate:
>
> Punctuality:
>
> useful　　　　　　　　　　　　　　　　　　useless
>
> 1　　2　　3　　4　　5　　6　　7　　8　　9　　10

Tool 3.2 shows different types of rating scales.

Ranking Scale

The purpose of a *ranking* survey question is to identify the importance of each item to the survey respondents, who indicate preferences by writing a number to show best to worst, most to least, and so forth. For example:

Predict job success for a new employee by giving each item a sequential number from 1 to 5):

_____ length of service on previous jobs

_____ no employment gaps on an application

_____ similar or increased salary in new job

_____ attendance record

_____ amount of vacation previously taken

[handwritten margin note: delete this approach — rank your own skills with these — 1–5; done.]

Short Answer

The purpose of a short answer question is to identify a unique opinion to an unprompted answer and to elicit complex ideas or a creative approach. Here are two examples:

What is the basis for the legal and illegal wording of questions asked in an employment interview?

What else would you like us to know about your team of two that would be helpful in planning this workshop?

Regardless of the type of question(s) selected for a written survey, be sure to make questions substantial or something of consequence. Avoid making the survey a difficult task by asking respondents to use correct grammar; write options of equal length; and limit the length of sentences to sixteen words. Avoid complex vocabulary and words with more than three syllables.

Tool 3.2. Types of Rating Scales

Following are different scales to measure performance. Depending on the specific skill being rated, these scales can be modified appropriately. In all of these rating scales, the higher numeric rating is considered a better score.

Quality

A quality rating scale assumes there is an acceptable standard of performance. Consider these types of rating scales to measure *how well* or *how correctly* a skill is performed.

How Well a Skill Is Performed

1 = Fails to meet standard

2 = Completes few steps correctly

3 = Meets most requirements

4 = All steps done correctly

5 = Exceeds standard and meets all standards

How Correctly a Skill Is Performed

1 = Did not use appropriate people, tools, materials

2 = Skill partially completed

3 = Skill completed correctly

4 = Skill completed correctly under prescribed conditions

5 = Skill completed correctly under prescribed conditions

Training Needs Assessment. Copyright © 2006 by Jean Barbazette. Reproduced by permission of Pfeiffer, an Imprint of Wiley. www.pfeiffer.com

Tool 3.2. Types of Rating Scales, Cont'd

Quantity

A quantity rating scale assumes there is a minimum standard of performance. Use this type of rating scale to measure how often the step is done.

1 = Step is not performed

2 = Step is done once

3 = Step is done required number of times

4 = Step is done more often than required by the standard

Speed

A speed rating scale assumes there is a minimum or maximum standard of performance. Use this type of rating scale to measure how rapidly the step is done.

1 = Step is done too slowly

2 = Step is done too quickly

3 = Step is done to standard

4 = Step positively exceeds standard

Sequence

A sequence rating scale assumes there is a standard order of steps for the process. Use this type of rating scale to measure whether the prescribed order of steps is followed.

1 = Prescribed sequence of steps was not followed

2 = Several steps performed out of sequence

3 = One step performed out of sequence

4 = All steps performed in the prescribed sequence

Training Needs Assessment. Copyright © 2006 by Jean Barbazette. Reproduced by permission of Pfeiffer, an Imprint of Wiley. www.pfeiffer.com

Tool 3.2. Types of Rating Scales, Cont'd

Perception

These rating scales ask the respondent to identify the intensity of different feelings.

Comfort

1. Extremely comfortable and open

2. Comfortable

3. Comfortable but guarded

4. Guarded and defensive

Confidence

1. Extremely confident

2. Very confident

3. Somewhat confident

4. Little confidence

Level of Success

1. Completely

2. Mostly successful

3. Partially successful

4. Failed to complete

Fairness

1. Fair, impartial, and consistent

2. Fair and impartial, not always consistent

3. Consistent, sometimes unfair

4. Sometimes has favorites

Training Needs Assessment. Copyright © 2006 by Jean Barbazette. Reproduced by permission of Pfeiffer, an Imprint of Wiley. www.pfeiffer.com

Tool 3.2. Types of Rating Scales, Cont'd

Excellence

1. Excellent
2. Good
3. Fair
4. Poor

Frequency

1. Daily
2. Twice a week
3. Weekly
4. As needed

Ease

1. Extremely easy
2. Somewhat easy
3. Somewhat difficult
4. Extremely difficult

Length

1. Just right
2. Too long
3. Too short

Clarity

1. All were clear
2. Most were clear
3. Some were clear
4. Very confusing

Training Needs Assessment. Copyright © 2006 by Jean Barbazette. Reproduced by permission of Pfeiffer, an Imprint of Wiley. www.pfeiffer.com

---

Tool 3.2. Types of Rating Scales, Cont'd

Agreement (1)

1. Agree with all

2. Agree with most, disagree with a few

3. Agree with some, disagree with most

4. Disagree with all

Agreement (2)

1. Strongly agree

2. Agree

3. Neutral

4. Disagree

5. Strongly disagree

Training Needs Assessment. Copyright © 2006 by Jean Barbazette. Reproduced by permission of Pfeiffer, an Imprint of Wiley. www.pfeiffer.com

---

Figures 3.1 and 3.2 are examples of a ranking survey completed by teams of two. Figure 3.1 is the manager's version of the survey and Figure 3.2 is the administrative assistant's version of the survey. The purpose of the survey is to identify what tasks an administrative assistant currently completes, which is recorded in column A. Column B records to what extent this behavior is desired in the future. After the information is collected, the differences in perceptions by each part of the team of two are analyzed to determine what type of training program would benefit these teams.

Figure 3.3 is a comparison of the survey results from managers and administrative assistants. Figure 3.4 is the cover memo that accompanied the survey. Interpretations from the survey results follow the survey data.

Figure 3.1. Team of Two Survey (Manager Version)

Directions: Use these scales to rate each column:

Column A Rating:

Current Behavior

4 = definitely does this

3 = somewhat does this

2 = rarely does this

1 = does not do this

Column B Rating:

Future Behavior

4 = strongly encourage my assistant to do this

3 = slightly encourage

2 = slightly discourage my assistant

1 = strongly discourage my assistant

Column A: Current Behavior	Column B: Future Behavior	Administrative Support Person Behavior
		1. Anticipate manager's needs
		2. Takes initiative with repetitive tasks
		3. Functions as the manager's buffer or go-between
		4. Knows manager's priorities and acts on them without added direction
		5. Knows how multiple activities and decisions fit together and focuses activity according to manager's priorities
		6. Is expert at tasks in own functional area
		7. Adapts to or initiates changes
		8. Knows how to get things done both through formal channels and informal networks
		9. Understands the origin and reasoning behind key policies, practices, and procedures
		10. Reads all available communication for the business and department
		11. Sometimes acts as the manager's surrogate
		12. Routinely completes complex tasks like monitoring budgets, managing multiple projects, managing and influencing others
		13. Takes initiative to research complex tasks
		14. Proposes alternative actions and makes suggestions
		15. Acts as sounding board for the manager
		16. Accurately scopes out length and difficulty of tasks and projects
		17. Anticipates and adjusts for problems and roadblocks

Figure 3.1. Team of Two Survey (Manager Version), Cont'd

Column A: Current Behavior	Column B: Future Behavior	Administrative Support Person Behavior
		18. Quickly grasps the essence and the underlying structure of situations
		19. Understands how to separate and combine tasks into efficient workflow
		20. Balances concurrent activities and meets deadlines

Number of years with this company _____

Number of years in a manager position _____

Number of years working with this administrative assistant _____

What else would you like us to know about your team of two that would be helpful in planning this workshop? _____

_____

Figure 3.2. Team of Two Survey (Administrative Assistant Version)

Directions: Use these scales to rate each column:

Column A Rating: **Current Behavior**	**Column B Rating:** **Future Behavior**
4 = definitely do this	4 = strongly encouraged to do this
3 = somewhat do this	3 = slightly encouraged
2 = rarely do this	2 = slightly discouraged
1 = do not do this	1 = strongly discouraged

Column A: Current Behavior	Column B: Future Behavior	Administrative Support Person Behavior
		1. You anticipate your manager's needs
		2. You take initiative with repetitive tasks
		3. You function as the manager's buffer or go-between
		4. You know manager's priorities and act on them without added direction

Figure 3.2. Team of Two Survey (Administrative Assistant Version), Cont'd

Column A: Current Behavior	Column B: Future Behavior	Administrative Support Person Behavior
		5. You know how multiple activities and decisions fit together and focus activity according to your manager's priorities
		6. You are expert at tasks in own functional area
		7. You adapt to or initiate changes
		8. You know how to get things done both through formal channels and the informal networks
		9. You understand the origin and reasoning behind key policies, practices, and procedures
		10. You read all available communication for the business and department
		11. You sometimes act as the manager's surrogate
		12. You routinely complete complex tasks like monitoring budgets, managing multiple projects, managing and influencing others
		13. You take initiative to research complex tasks
		14. You propose alternative actions and make suggestions
		15. You act as a sounding board for the manager
		16. You accurately scope out length and difficulty of tasks and projects
		17. You anticipate and adjust for problems and roadblocks
		18. You quickly grasp the essence and the underlying structure of situations
		19. You understand how to separate and combine tasks into efficient workflow
		20. You balance concurrent activities and meet deadlines

Number of years with the company _____

Number of years in an administrative position _____

Number of years working with this manager _____

What else would you like us to know about your team of two that would be helpful in planning this workshop? _____
_____

Figure 3.3. Sample Survey Results and Trends

Directions: Use these scales to rate each column:

Column A Rating:
Current Behavior

Column B Rating:
Future Behavior

4 = strongly encourage my assistant to do this

3 = slightly encourage

2 = slightly discourage my assistant

1 = strongly discourage my assistant

4 = definitely does this

3 = somewhat does this

2 = rarely does this

1 = does not do this

Scores reported here are an average of the fifty managers and thirty-two administrative assistants who responded to the survey. This represents a 67 percent response.

Column A: Current Behavior Manager	Column A: Current Behavior Admin	Column B: Future Behavior Manager	Column B: Future Behavior Admin	Administrative support person behavior
3.6	3.7	3.8	4.0	1. Anticipate manager's needs
3.8	3.8	3.8	3.8	2. Takes initiative with repetitive tasks
2.5	2.8	3.1	3.7	3. Functions as the manager's buffer or go-between
3.7	3.8	3.7	3.8	4. Knows manager's priorities and acts on them without added direction
3.0	3.7	3.6	3.7	5. Knows how multiple activities and decisions fit together and focuses activity according to manager's priorities
3.9	3.8	3.9	3.8	6. Is expert at tasks in own functional area
3.0	3.4	3.3	3.7	7. Adapts to or initiates changes

Figure 3.3. Sample Survey Results and Trends, Cont'd

Column A: Current Behavior Manager	Column A: Current Behavior Admin	Column B: Future Behavior Manager	Column B: Future Behavior Admin	Administrative support person behavior
3.8	3.9	3.8	3.9	8. Knows how to get things done both through formal channels and the informal network
2.5	3.2	3.0	3.5	9. Understands the origin and reasoning behind key policies, practices, and procedures
2.2	3.0	2.8	3.4	10. Reads all available communication for the business and department
2.5	2.6	3.3	3.1	11. Sometimes acts as the manager's surrogate
2.9	3.2	3.2	3.8	12. Routinely completes complex tasks like monitoring budgets, managing multiple projects, managing and influencing others
2.8	3.2	3.1	3.6	13. Takes initiative to research complex tasks
3.0	3.3	3.3	3.6	14. Proposes alternative actions and makes suggestions
2.0	3.0	2.7	3.4	15. Acts as sounding board for the manager
2.5	3.1	2.9	3.3	16. Accurately scopes out length and difficulty of tasks and projects
3.5	3.6	3.5	3.6	17. Anticipates and adjusts for problems and roadblocks
3.2	3.4	3.4	3.6	18. Quickly grasps the essence and the underlying structure of situations
3.2	3.8	3.6	3.9	19. Understands how to separate and combine tasks into efficient workflow
3.9	3.9	3.9	3.9	20. Balances concurrent activities and meets deadlines

Thirty-eight out of fifty managers have had the support of their current admin for five years or less.
Twenty-two of the thirty-eight managers have had the support of their current admin for less than one year.

Figure 3.4. Cover Memo to Accompany Survey

Cover Memo

We are excited about a new program, Team of Two, which is designed to enhance the effectiveness of the manager/administrative assistant team.

The "Team of Two" program for Managers and Administrative Assistants will be launched in the fall. Since this is a bold and much-anticipated company-wide program, we are asking the Executive Team and the Executive Team Administrative Assistants from each function to participate in the pilot program during the third week of October. If your team of two would like to represent your function in the pilot program, please notify us of your interest.

Following the October pilot, additional workshops will be held between November and January of next year.

Our company is partnering with The Training Clinic to create a custom-designed program to meet the needs of our teams of two. The Training Clinic has been working with our administrative staff by presenting half-day workshops over the past two years.

We ask your help in customizing this program by completing the attached two-page survey. Two versions of the survey are attached: one for managers and one for administrative assistants. They refer to the same dimensions and will help identify how your current team functions and what the future might look like. We appreciate your willingness to complete this brief survey. It is not intended to be an evaluation of administrative assistant performance.

Please complete the survey separately, without consulting the other part of your team of two. Trust your first reaction when completing the survey. There are no "right" answers. We're looking for TRENDS in current practices and opinions.

After completing the survey anonymously, return it by mail or email or fax it to The Training Clinic by [insert an appropriate date].

What Are Guidelines to Collect Statistically Significant Information?

When conducting surveys of employees or customers to identify training issues, it is important to include enough of the target population so that, when results are tabulated from the returned surveys, the results will be correct for the entire population. For example, if the target population is one hundred people and only ten surveys are returned, the chances of the ten returned surveys accurately representing the opinions of the other ninety people are very low, or not statistically significant. If, however, seventy surveys are returned, the chances are higher that the opinions of the thirty unreturned surveys are probably similar to those expressed by the seventy survey respondents.

Therefore, the higher the return rate for survey completion, the more accurately the survey results will represent the opinions of the entire group. The survey results shown in Figure 3.3 represent 67 percent of the target population of 120 employees. There is no doubt some opinions are not represented by the missing 33 percent. The task force made decisions based on the information available at the time. This explanation of statistical significance is a simple one. Readers who have more interest in this topic, please see the references in the bibliography of this book.

When and Why Are Interviews Appropriate to Gather Information?

When groups of employees are small in number, it is easier to interview most of them, rather than conduct a survey. For a group of over fifty people, it may be helpful to conduct a few interviews to get a sense of the group and what issues they are likely to raise. A survey can easily follow interviews to identify how widely held the opinions expressed in some of the interviews are. Availability of employees for interviews may also limit the ability to conduct a one-on-one interview.

Prior to the Interview

To gain the cooperation of the person being interviewed, cover several items when you make the appointment for the interview. Share the purpose of the interview and why this person's information is vital to the topic. Limit the interview to thirty minutes for line employees and no more than sixty minutes for even the most interested person. Set aside a quiet and private space for the interview so you will avoid distractions and interruptions. If the interview contains complex questions, consider sharing the questions prior to the interview so the respondent has an opportunity to think of the answers to your questions. Make clear to the person answering your questions whether the information you collect is anonymous (the source of remarks will not be known) or confidential (what is said will not be reported, but only used as background information).

Types of Interview Questions

Plan questions for the interview ahead of time. Write open-ended questions that will meet the purpose of the interview. Open-ended questions usually begin with "what," "why," or "how." The questions asked in interviews change with the objective or purpose of the interview. For example, sample basic and follow-up interview questions follow from the Team of Two assessment example shown earlier in this chapter.

Basic Interview Questions

- What does your team do to promote communication?
- What barriers get in the way of holding your daily meetings?
- What would help you overcome communication barriers?
- What are techniques your team would like to try to be more effective?
- What is stopping you from trying better ways to communicate?

Follow-Up Interview Questions

- What else can you tell me about that?
- How have you handled similar issues?
- What other concerns do you have?
- What are other examples of that?
- What else has happened when. . . ?
- Why do you think that happened?
- Has anyone else had that same or a similar experience?

Interview Next Steps

Following the interview, write a summary of important points. Summarize the information learned into themes related to the objective or purpose of the interview. Identify issues that need more investigation. Make an initial interpretation of the meaning of the information collected. Chapter 10 discusses how to summarize information into a training plan. Chapters 4 through 9 contain different types of needs analysis. After we look at each type of analysis, how to interpret information, make recommendations, and write a training plan is addressed in Chapter 10.

CHAPTER 4

FEASIBILITY ANALYSIS

Chapter Objectives

- Identify why a feasibility analysis is done
- Identify how to estimate the benefit of training and compare it to the current cost of performance without training

Tools

- Cost/Benefit Analysis Template

Chapter Questions

- What is the purpose of a feasibility analysis?
- How is a feasibility analysis conducted?

What Is the Purpose of a Feasibility Analysis?

A feasibility analysis is a cost/benefit analysis completed prior to conducting training. It is an estimate of the cost of the training weighed against the possible benefits that could be achieved if training were conducted. A feasibility analysis identifies whether conducting the training costs less than doing nothing.

How Is a Feasibility Analysis Conducted?

When considering whether to conduct a training program to solve a performance problem, conduct a feasibility analysis for a specific program. As the example in Figure 4.1 shows, start by identifying training program information: name and class hours, the target population with the number of participants and number of sessions, the business-related objective for conducting the training, and the total participant learning hours (PLH). PLH is calculated by multiplying the number of participants by class hours. PLH is later divided into the total cost to find the cost per participant and cost per learning hour. The cost per learning hour, similar to a "man hour" figure, can be used to compare the cost of one training program to another. The business-related objective for the program is the bottom-line result sought by conducting the training—in this example, to reduce turnover of new hires by 20 percent.

In this model, costs and benefits are shown in two columns. Costs are listed to the left, benefits to the right. *Direct* costs are those related to conducting this specific program. Accounting departments can help you find similar cost information for your training programs. *Indirect* costs are general and administrative expenses or overhead expenses for the training function that are not identified with a specific training program. Indirect costs include telephone expense, administrative salary and fringe benefits, equipment maintenance costs, and so on. Calculate indirect expenses for a year and divide it equally among all training programs.

Some cost/benefit analyses show participant compensation for salary earned while the training is conducted. It is only appropriate to show participant compensation if participants produce revenue for the organization (such as salespeople) or participants need to be replaced while attending training. In Figure 4.1, for example, participants are store managers who needed to be replaced in order to attend training during work hours. Operating salary reports show salary figures for all store managers. The total for store managers' salaries is divided by the number of store managers to create an average daily salary rate.

The benefit column shows productivity figures, such as turnover and the cost to recruit, hire, orient, and train a new clerk. If the objective is reached and turnover is reduced by 20 percent, then the benefit is a net savings of $852,150. When the benefit ($900,000) is divided by the cost ($47,850) the cost/benefit ratio is 19:1. That means for every dollar invested in this training program, $19 are returned to the organization. Therefore, it is feasible economically to conduct the program. A cost/benefit ratio for a for-profit, publicly held organization needs to be at least the same as or better than the earnings per share of the organization's stock. Earnings-per-share is usually reported by publicly held companies on a quarterly basis. A cost/benefit ratio for a non-profit or government organization needs to be at least 1:1 to be feasible economically.

Another measure of economic feasibility is calculated through return on investment by taking the net savings and dividing it by the cost. In this example it is 1,781 percent.

Overview of Figure 4.1 Cost/Benefit Analysis

The cost/benefit analysis shown in Figure 4.1 is an example from a retail organization that wants to reduce turnover of entry-level clerks by training store managers to make better hiring decisions of employees by conducting a better selection interview.

Cost of Current Performance

A performance analysis of the current situation revealed that store managers frequently asked existing employees for referrals for job candidates, did not adequately screen job applications, and often conducted brief job interviews on the sales floor. These interviews usually lasted about five minutes, with the store manager deciding to use the thirty-day probationary period to confirm whether a good hiring "decision" was made. Sometimes the store manager's intuition was wrong and the new employee would be terminated during the first thirty days of employment. This hiring practice resulted in an average turnover rate of 75 percent. Usually, turnover statistics can be found in monthly operating reports.

Figure 4.1. Cost/Benefit Analysis Example

Training Program: Selection Interviewing (seven hours)

Target Population: 100 Retail Store Managers (three large group classes)

Objective: Reduce turnover of new hires by 20 percent

TOTAL PLH (participant learning hour) = 700 (Duration of 7 hours x number of participants or 100)

COST		BENEFIT
Direct Costs		**(Based on previous needs assessment)**
Course design	$9,000	Average turnover rate 75 percent
Instructor	2,500	
Slide-tape production	10,000	
Materials duplication	500	Average # clerks = 20
Travel/overnight for instructor	1,000	Cost to train a new clerk
Travel for participants	1,000	for 30 days = $3,000
Transparencies	50	
Meals, refreshments	3,000	15 new clerks/year x $3,000 =
		$45,000 **cost per store**
Total Direct Costs	$27,050	
Indirect Costs	800	$45,000 per store
		x 100 stores = $4,500,000 lost
Total Costs	$27,850	$4,500,000
		x .20 (target)
Participant Compensation	$20,000	$ 900,000 **benefit**
Total Cost	$47,850	$852,150 **net savings**

PLH cost is $68.36 = $47,850 (Total costs) ÷ 700 (PLH)

Program Cost per Participant is $478.50 = $47,850 ÷ 100 (number of participants)

Benefit $\frac{\$900,000}{\$47,850}$ = 19:1 CBR   Net Savings $\frac{\$852,150}{\$47,850}$ x 100 = 1781% ROI

The cost of recruiting, hiring, orienting, and training a new minimum wage employee in this organization is roughly $3,000. Costs for recruiting, hiring, and orienting new employees can also be extracted from operating reports. The cost of 75 percent turnover is about $45,000 per store per year. If this hiring practice is duplicated throughout the entire chain of one hundred stores, the cost could be as much as $4,500,000 per year.

Proposed Intervention to Improve Performance

The training plan proposed to conduct a *Selection Interviewing* workshop to provide skills for the managers, along with a few changes in recruitment practices and a revised job application. It was also recommended that store managers train their assistant store managers to screen candidate applications to save the store managers' time. Then the store managers would have more time to conduct a more thorough interview and make a better hiring decision.

Cost of Proposed Training

The cost/benefit objective of the intervention was to reduce turnover by 20 percent. Since there are several factors that can influence turnover, a modest target of 20 percent could be attributed to the successful intervention. If this objective were achieved, a projected benefit in one year would be $900,000.

Calculating ROI

Since the cost of the training is $47,850, including participant compensation, the cost/benefit ratio is 19:1. This means that for every training dollar spent, the return is more than $19 back to the organization. This is a very high rate of return and suggests it is economically feasible to conduct this training.

To actually calculate the return on investment (ROI), this analysis needs to be calculated a second time, after the training has been conducted. This example and the explanation in this chapter is a simplified approach to calculating ROI. The bibliography at the end of this book list more complete references for calculating cost/benefit analysis and ROI. A template for a feasibility (cost-benefit) analysis is shown in Tool 4.1.

Once you have determined that it is feasible economically, and you have determined through a performance analysis that you will address a training issue, the next step in needs assessment is to tie the proposed training to a business need. The next chapter discusses how to sort training *wants* from training *needs* by relating the training needs to a business need.

Tool 4.1. Cost/Benefit Analysis Template

Training Program:_____

Target Population:_____

Business Need/Objective:_____

Total Participant Learning Hour (PLH) = duration x number
of participants:_____

Cost/Investment		Benefit as Cost Reduction
Direct Costs		Performance indicator** before
Course design	_____	training times number of
Instructor	_____	personnel = current cost
AV materials production	_____	Performance indicator after
Travel/overnight: Instructor	_____	training times number of
Travel: Participants	_____	personnel = new cost
Transparencies	_____	Current cost less new
Meals, refreshments	_____	cost = benefit of training
Total Direct Costs	_____	
		Benefits as Revenue Increase
Indirect Costs	_____	Level of revenue generated by
		target population before training
Subtotal: Total direct and		subtracted from level of revenue
indirect costs	_____	generated by target population
Participant Compensation	_____	after training = revenue increase
		(benefit of training)
Total Cost	_____	

PLH costs (Total costs ÷ PLH) = _____

Program cost per participant = total cost ÷ number of participants) =_____

Benefit ÷ Total Costs = Net Savings

Return on Investment = Benefits ÷ Costs

**What costs are associated with poor performance? What is the indicator of current cost of
performance?

Training Needs Assessment. Copyright © 2006 by Jean Barbazette. Reproduced by permission of
Pfeiffer, an Imprint of Wiley. www.pfeiffer.com

CHAPTER 5

NEEDS VERSUS WANTS ANALYSIS

Chapter Objectives

- Learn about survey techniques
- Learn about individual interviews
- See how to interpret survey information
- Learn how to make recommendations from data

Tools

- Sample Needs Versus Wants Survey

Chapter Questions

- What is a needs versus wants survey?
- How is it conducted?
- Who should do it and how to interpret results?

What Is a Needs Versus Wants Survey?

This type of analysis identifies training needs that are related to the organization's business. Training is linked to the bottom line, and providing appropriate training will benefit the individual as well as the organization.

It is often difficult for individuals to distinguish between what training they *need* to improve specific skill areas related to a business and training that they *want* or would like to complete that fills other needs, both personal and professional. For example, an individual might *want* to take a course in computer graphics, but may not *need* to use this skill in a current job.

How Is It Conducted?

Prior to conducting a survey, interview a few of the target population for their comments about their work and ask them to offer suggestions for training. Following is a sample list of questions to ask of supervisors about their current job practices and performance. The consultant asking questions makes notes of the supervisor's answers during individual or group interviews. A summary of their comments follows later in this chapter. After an interview, circulate a written survey to sort out needs versus wants of the target population (supervisors in this example).

Interview Questions

- How long have you been a supervisor?
- Are all supervisors promoted because they were high-performing employees or are some supervisors hired from outside the organization?
- What are the characteristics of a "good" supervisor?
- Describe your typical day.
- What do you like and dislike about your job?
- Are there any unusual circumstances that impact work right now? If so, what are they?
- What prior training have you had to develop supervisory skills?

- What issues or problems make it difficult for you to do your job well?
- What type of support do you get from management when dealing with your subordinates?
- How can management better support your work?
- What type of training would help you be a more effective supervisor?

It is most appropriate to survey more than two levels in the organization to obtain more than one point of view. Identify one level of employees who are the appropriate target audience for skill development, for example, front-line supervisors, as in the example above. Ask the supervisors what skills they need to meet their current responsibilities and what skills their peer group needs to complete their responsibilities more effectively. It may also be appropriate to survey the subordinates of those supervisors and perhaps their managers.

When more than two perspectives are used to identify training needs, the "wants" or personal desires are easily spotted and true training needs can be addressed.

Tool 5.1 is an example of a survey used to assess the training needs of a specific group of supervisors. The survey was given to supervisors, and another slightly modified survey was given to their subordinates. Supervisors were asked for their preferences in the "you" column and for the preferences of their peers in the "all other supervisors" column. It was appropriate for supervisors to rate their peers, since most had been working together for some time and were aware of strengths and weaknesses in their peers. When circulating a survey with course titles, provide a course description to give a common understanding of course content. List only those courses that an organization is prepared to offer. If a course is listed in a survey, then the expectation is that the course will be offered if enough employees request it. Sometimes a fourth area is assessed that lists technical job skills, such as "Inventory Software Training" or "Financial Skills." In this example, no technical skills are listed, since all supervisors were promoted from within because of their excellent technical skills.

Tool 5.1. Sample Needs Versus Wants Survey

To All Supervisors: Rank the following courses first, second, and third on the basis of how much benefit they would be to you and to other supervisors in our company. Do this for each of three skill areas in each column. You will have six groupings of first, second, and third choices. Please read course descriptions before making choices.

	You	All Other Supervisors
Personal Skills (Rank 1st, 2nd, 3rd)		
Active Listening	_____	_____
Oral Presentations	_____	_____
Personal Computer Skills	_____	_____
Problem Solving and Decision Making	_____	_____
Stress Management	_____	_____
Time Management	_____	_____
Interpersonal Skills (Rank 1st, 2nd, 3rd)		
Business Writing	_____	_____
Coaching and Counseling	_____	_____
Conflict Management	_____	_____
Dealing with Internal/External Customers	_____	_____
Effective Communication	_____	_____
Meeting Management	_____	_____
Motivation	_____	_____
Self-Directed Work Teams	_____	_____
Team Building	_____	_____
Supervision Skills (Rank 1st, 2nd, 3rd)		
Delegation	_____	_____
Goal Setting	_____	_____

Tool 5.1. Sample Needs Versus Wants Survey, Cont'd

	You	All Other Supervisors
Labor Relations	_____	_____
Leadership and Empowerment	_____	_____
Managing Change	_____	_____
Performance Appraisal	_____	_____
Progressive Discipline	_____	_____
Selection Interviewing	_____	_____
Training Subordinates	_____	_____

What would help you become more effective and advance your career goals? What is the biggest threat to your success as a supervisor?

_____

Training Needs Assessment. Copyright © 2006 by Jean Barbazette. Reproduced by permission of Pfeiffer, an Imprint of Wiley. www.pfeiffer.com

---

The two questions listed at the bottom of the survey are asked to help identify additional needs not addressed in the courses listed in the survey and to identify other factors that could impact training. Generally, survey respondents give three types of answers to these questions. First, respondents say they are not threatened. This is a healthy answer for an organization. Second, respondents say they have made past mistakes that could be held against them. This is also a healthy answer that shows an interest in self-improvement. Third, respondents blame others for lack of success. This type of "victim" answer is not healthy for an organization. For example, a respondent could claim nepotism or others "don't like him" or the manager "plays favorites." However, when more than 5 percent of respondents blame others, no amount of training will ensure success in this organization. Other interventions besides training are needed to remedy this type of situation. For example, putting promotion policies in writing and clarifying the job posting process may be ways to address nepotism or favoritism issues.

Figure 5.1 is a sample summary of survey results and identifies the top three or four most-requested courses selected by three groups. A weighting system was used to identify the top three or four requested courses. A course rated "1" was given 5 points; a course rated "2" was given 3 points; and a course rated "3" was given 1 point. When all the points for specific courses were totaled, the top three or four courses emerged. Raw points were not reported as part of the survey, since the objective was to identify the most frequently requested courses.

Twenty of the thirty supervisors in the target population were also interviewed after completing the survey. The remaining supervisors were not available because of vacations, shift timing, and schedule changes. The twenty-five supervisors also completed a written survey. Thirty-five percent of the assembly workers also completed a written survey. Upper management did not complete a survey and were the feedback group to whom the consultant reported the results. Only informal on-the-job training has been done for the supervisors by the managers to this point. Narrative survey comments from the supervisor and their subordinates follow Figure 5.1.

After reviewing the survey results and narrative comments, try to guess which four training programs management selected in this case. Then read the rationale for management's decisions to select four training programs for this group and reflect their needs, rather than what they said they wanted.

Figure 5.1. Example of Supervisory Development Survey Results

Supervisors Say "I need . . ."	Other Supervisors Need . . .	Workers Say Supervisors Need . . .
Personal Skills	**Personal Skills**	**Personal Skills**
Time Management	Time Management	Problem Solving and Decision Making
Problem Solving and Decision Making	Active Listening	Active Listening
Stress Management	Problem Solving and Decision Making	Time Management
Interpersonal Skills	**Interpersonal Skills**	**Interpersonal Skills**
Coaching/Counseling	Team Building	Team Building
Motivation	Motivation	Effective Communication
Team Building	Coaching/Counseling	Motivation
Effective Communication		Conflict Management
Supervisory Skills	**Supervisory Skills**	**Supervisory Skills**
Leadership Styles	Goal Setting	Leadership Styles
Training Subordinates	Leadership Styles	Labor Relations
Goal Setting	Training Subordinates	Delegation

Comments from Supervisors

"It's pretty busy around here right now. I don't know if there is any time to attend a training class. You know, I've been at this job and in this business for over twenty-five years."

"I really have some trouble keeping the newer guys in line. If you give them an inch, they take a mile. I try to be patient, but if you don't kick them a little, the work never gets done. It seems that I need to be everywhere at one time."

"—is really a good manager to work for. You going to tell him I said that? He could listen a bit more to our problems. There is just too much overtime right now. Everything is a rush. I go home tired; I wake up tired. It's not fun to come to work anymore the way it used to be."

"The union is pretty good. But there are some guys who are always complaining about being singled out for discipline. I let them know right away what's wrong and how to fix it. Are we really going to have some training? That would be great. The other guys really need the help."

"How about not so much negative criticism? We occasionally hear about the good job we do, but there is never a comment on the small things. I've been in the same place for two years now. There is such pressure to catch up . . . all this overtime . . . my family just doesn't understand the pressure or the career opportunity that can come from it."

"I'd like to be able to spend more time with new people. There just never seems to be enough time to show them what's expected and how to do it right."

Comments from Assembly Line Workers

"It would really help my boss to listen before he climbs all over my case. I'd like some help from him—instead of him always trying to write someone up. He thinks he's a real tough guy."

"I've seen an improvement in communication in the last month. That's the key to everything. We need more of that."

"Supervisors need to get more done through the foreman. Give each foreman an area to be responsible for instead of trying to do everything himself. This would free up your supervisors to make decisions, effect meaningful planning, and be more knowledgeable about all areas of the line."

"Supervisors need to have a more positive attitude. They are kinda suspicious, most of the time. A little praise for a job well done would be appreciated."

"In the past my supervisor has had a double standard. He's also not very good at listening."

"The supervisors are under constant and excessive pressure and lack understanding from upper management about what really goes on down here."

"My supervisor lacks confidence. He changes his mind too easily."

"Maybe asking questions before jumping to conclusions about what has and has not been done, and who did it."

"More positive attitude toward labor relations."

"Act on employees' suggestions. Delegating more authority to us would create more harmony."

Who Should Do It and How to Interpret Results?

The needs assessor, often with a management group, will identify which are actual training *needs* and which are *wants* that ought not receive scarce training resources. In the example provided, the needs assessor met with the general manager and five senior managers of the supervisors to discuss the survey results. Here is the rationale for the top four courses this organization selected as a result of the survey.

When reviewing the survey results, it makes sense to consider workshops recommended by all three groups, such as "Time Management" or "Problem Solving and Decision Making." The needs assessor asked the management group to explain whether or not the supervisors were disorganized and what might prompt a request for time management training. The managers said that there was a temporary increase in the workload and the time pressures for supervisors would fade away in a month or less when the group would be fully staffed. So even though supervisors *wanted* time management training, it wasn't *needed.* Requests for time management are often symptoms of other needs.

It is not unusual for supervisors and their subordinates to identify the same need, but to "name it" as something different. The example in Figure 5.1 shows supervisors and their peers suggest that training in goal setting is a need. The subordinates recommend that supervisors be given training in labor relations. When supervisors have attempted to use collaborative goal-setting techniques, the subordinates suggest that the supervisors don't understand their labor contract. Workers think collaborative goal setting is inappropriate, since working conditions have already been negotiated by their union representatives. Both levels of employees surveyed were describing the same issue, but naming it differently from their own perspectives.

The four workshops selected by the management group for the supervisors included:

1. Leadership Skills

2. Effective Communication

3. Problem Solving and Decision Making

4. Motivation and Discipline

Since few of the supervisors had received any training for leading others, a "Leadership Skills" workshop was offered as the foundation for skill development. No communication skills had been offered to the group, so this was the second workshop along with some "Active Listening" skills. It is interesting that few individuals ever request listening skills training for themselves, while it is frequently recommended for others. At the end of the "Effective Communication" workshop, supervisors were asked by the trainer what types of problems they wanted addressed in the "Problem Solving and Decision Making" workshop. Most of the problems mentioned had to do with motivating subordinates and handling discipline in an assertive manner. With that additional information, the "Problem Solving and Decision Making" workshop was moved from the third workshop to the end of the sequence.

A few other classes might be considered as a *need* rather than a *want.* "Team Building" was considered by the management group as a possible workshop. However, since the supervisors had difficulty communicating effectively, "Team Building" was beyond the basic level *needed* by the supervisors.

By using survey information from three points of view and discussing the results with yet another level of employees (managers), the needs assessor was able to help management sort out the training *needs* from what the employees *wanted*. The four workshops were related to increasing the productivity and morale of the subordinates.

If you have completed a performance analysis, feasibility analysis, and needs versus wants analysis, then you are dealing with an issue that can be remedied by training. You can save the organization money if deficient performance is corrected and is definitely related to a business need. The next type of analysis to think about conducting is *goal analysis*. A goal analysis is appropriate to define the need in concrete and specific terms so the results of the training are clearly related to a business need.

GOAL ANALYSIS

Chapter Objectives

- Identify the purpose of goal analysis
- Learn how to conduct a goal analysis
- Write a sample goal analysis statement

Tool

- Goal Analysis Template

Chapter Questions

- What is the purpose of goal analysis?
- How is it conducted?

What Is the Purpose of Goal Analysis?

The purpose of goal analysis is to make a vague performance desire more specific and measurable through a consensus process. Goal analysis is conducted in response to a client's request for improved performance that is originally described in vague or attitudinal terms. For example, a performance improvement goal may be described as "Let's make our salespeople more professional," "Let's encourage our customer service representatives to be more empathetic and understanding," or "Let's have our analysts work smarter, not harder." While each of these three performance improvement goals is important, they often mean different results to different people. In order to meet these goals, first develop specific objectives that are measurable and time-bound and have shared meaning between the client and the trainer.

How Is It Conducted?

Begin to conduct a goal analysis by discussing with the client which specific behaviors meet the performance goal. If needed, survey various stakeholders individually and ask for clarification of the goal from their points of view. As an option to individual surveys or interviews, ask a group to meet as a task force and more specifically describe the goal. While the group option is more time-consuming, the synergy from the group might generate a more specific goal and is worth the extra time.

Below are five steps needed to create a useful goal statement:

1. Create an initial *written* "SMART" goal statement that specifies and summarizes the desired outcome in behavioral terms. SMART goals are

   S = specific

   M = measurable

   A = agreed on

   R = realistic

   T = time-bound

For example, "If our customer service representatives were to become more professional, they would call the customer by name, actively listen to the customer's needs, identify the appropriate solution, gain the customer's agreement on the solution, and follow up. Each representative would complete a minimum of five calls per hour. This goal will be reviewed for completion in two weeks."

2. Brainstorm with a task force or individuals the specific performances that would indicate improved customer service or professionalism.

3. Prioritize this list through consensus discussion.

4. Write a draft goal statement to summarize the goal from the task force's discussion. The suggested format for a goal statement is: "If our salespeople [insert name of target population] were to become more professional [insert desired behavior or attitude], they would do . . . [list performances]. Each representative would complete a minimum of [give number] [list time frame or standard for performance]. This goal will be reviewed for completion in [list when goal will be reviewed]."

5. Test the draft written statement. Ask task force members or stakeholders if the target group were to do these things, would they be considered professional, more empathetic, or exactly what [insert goal]? Are all the dimensions of a SMART goal in the written statement?

While the concept of SMART goals has been used for more than thirty years when creating performance goals, using a SMART goal statement as the basis for goal analysis is an innovation. Once the goal analysis is complete, it can now become the basis for developing a training program to meet the goal. Each of the behaviors or performances listed in the goal statement can be taught to the target population as part of a training program.

Use Tool 6.1 as a template for goal analysis.

Tool 6.1. Goal Analysis Template

1. Write the target population and attribute for improvement:

   Make _____ [target population] more _____ [attribute].

2. Brainstorm a list of behaviors that could be observed if the target population possessed this attribute (behaviors can be stated in positive and/or negative terms . . . what is done or not done).

Do	Do Not Do
•	•
•	•
•	•
•	•
•	•
•	•
•	•
•	•
•	•
•	•
•	•

Training Needs Assessment. Copyright © 2006 by Jean Barbazette. Reproduced by permission of Pfeiffer, an Imprint of Wiley. www.pfeiffer.com

---

Tool 6.1. Goal Analysis Template, Cont'd

3. Prioritize the performances from most to least important.

4. Write a draft goal statement following this format: "If our [insert name of target population] were to become more [insert desired behavior or attitude], they would do . . . [list performances from point 2 above]. Each representative would complete a minimum of [insert desired number] [list time frame or standard for performance]. This goal will be reviewed for completion in [list when goal will be reviewed]."

5. Test the draft written statement. Ask task force members or stakeholders if the target group were to do these things, would they be considered more [insert goal]. Are all the dimensions of a SMART goal in the written statement?

Training Needs Assessment. Copyright © 2006 by Jean Barbazette. Reproduced by permission of Pfeiffer, an Imprint of Wiley. www.pfeiffer.com

---

The next type of analysis is task analysis. Chapter 7 discusses how to complete a task analysis.

7

TASK ANALYSIS

Chapter Objectives

- Break down a task into teachable parts
- Assess difficulty of completing the task
- Learn how to complete a skill hierarchy from a task analysis
- Identify prerequisites for learning a task

Tools

- Task Analysis Observation Template

Chapter Questions

- What is the purpose of task analysis?
- What is the difference between job analysis and task analysis?
- How is it conducted?
- What makes conducting task analysis difficult?
- What is done with the results of a task analysis?

What Is the Purpose of Task Analysis?

The purpose of task analysis is to find the best method to perform a task and the best sequence of steps to complete a specific task. For example, the customer service representative's goal from the previous chapter is to answer a customer's inquiry or request. Before deciding how to teach a customer service representative how to complete all parts of this task, conduct a task analysis by completing six steps that break down a task into its "teachable" parts. A task analysis can flow chart steps or list steps sequentially. Often task analysis is conducted to find the best method to complete a task or to force consistency in how a task is done throughout an organization.

What Is the Difference Between Job Analysis and Task Analysis?

A task is part of a job. Before conducting a task analysis, identify the different tasks that are part of a specific job. The process to analyze either a job or a task is the same. This chapter addresses task analysis. See the Bibliography at the end of the book for references about job and task analysis. Continuing with the customer service representative (CSR) example from the previous chapter, the CSR job contains many tasks; one task is to answer a customer's inquiry or request.

How Is It Conducted?

Complete a task analysis using these six steps:

1. *Observe the task* as it is done by a typical performer. Record your observation by listing task steps and estimate task difficulty for the typical performer. This will help you decide how much training is needed to develop task competence. Identify and write the skills needed to complete each step. A sample task breakdown is in Figure 7.1. A template to complete a task breakdown is given in Tool 7.1. Some documentation might already exist in standard operating procedure (SOP) manuals or other written job aids. Review the existing documentation prior to making an observation of the task and compare how the procedure is completed versus what the written documentation states. Ask the person you observe to

give you a rationale for differences you see. Ask the typical performer to identify how often the task is done in the manner observed and how often exceptions are likely to occur. Sort out what is typical and what is unusual when completing this task. In the CSR example, listen to actual or recorded calls to get an idea of the steps in answering a customer's call.

2. *Interview a master performer.* Try to validate easy and difficult steps in the task, and elicit any "tricks of the trade" previously used to teach this task to a new person. Master performers are often used as on-the-job trainers of new employees. Master performers can provide a wealth of information that can become job aids or teaching aids when this task is taught by a trainer. Senior CSRs can be helpful in pointing out shortcuts or offering questions they have used to get customers to relate the substance of a request more easily.

3. *Interview the boss/supervisor* of the typical performer. Validate the easy and difficult parts of the task and identify any perceived differences in how the task "ought" to be done versus what has been observed and recorded. Ask the supervisor to identify how they judge performance for CSRs. Ask the supervisor how often different types of requests or complaints are made. Be aware that how the task is done may have changed since the supervisor actually did this task.

4. *Use a task force* to identify regional differences and develop support for the standardization of the task to be taught, or get ideas from external experts on how to do this task correctly. If the task is completed locally, a task force might not be needed to accurately identify the best method of completing this task. In the CSR example, the organization may have more than one call center. Call centers might be located in different states or countries, depending on the nature of the organization. If that is the case, identify regional differences.

5. *Brainstorm with the target population.* Validate the easy and difficult parts of the task and any special problems associated with learning this task. Identify contingencies that may not have occurred to you yet. Ask a range of average to outstanding performers to brainstorm about the task. Find out how often different types of requests are taken by CSRs. Ask what type of feedback CSRs receive from their supervisors. Identify differences in how the task is done.

6. *Validate all of the above with a final observation.* Identify whether the initial observation is correct. From all that has been seen, recorded,and analyzed, decide the best way to teach this task to another person. Gain agreement from your client as to this "best" method to complete the task. Gaining agreement is important when the client wants consistent performance.

If the person conducting the job/task analysis is also the subject-matter expert, modify this process by writing Steps 1 and 2 and perhaps 4.

What Makes Conducting a Task Analysis Difficult?

Sometimes it is difficult to conduct a task analysis if the needs assessor is not familiar with the task that is observed. The novice assessor often has difficulty distinguishing a typical step in a task from an unusual step. Accurately assessing task difficulty can also be problematic. That's why observing and interviewing subject-matter experts, master performers, and typical target population representatives is critical to making an accurate observation. Be sure to break down the task into elementary parts that even a novice performer will understand.

Conversely, those who are very familiar with the task might be "unconsciously competent" (having little awareness of one's skill) or have the "disease of familiarity" (doing a task so often a difficult task becomes simple). Unconscious competence comes from doing a task so well that it becomes a habit. The performer is not consciously aware of issues a new performer might face. The performer is so familiar with the task that several assumed basic skills are not evident. These two "maladies" can lead to combining or eliminating other viewpoints about how to complete the task most appropriately. Again, break down the task into its elementary parts to overcome making assumptions.

What Is Done with the Results of a Task Analysis?

After completing a task analysis using the six steps described earlier in this chapter, the needs assessor usually creates a skill hierarchy of the task to completely document the observed steps collected on the Task Analysis Observation Template. An example of a skill hierarchy is given in Figure 7.2. Start by writing a learning objective for the task. How to write learning objectives and other course design issues will be covered in a later book in *The Skilled Trainer* series.

Figure 7.1. Sample Task Analysis Observation

Task: Answer a customer call

Steps	Skills	Task difficulty* 1 = easy 5 = hard
Answer the call	• Press telephone line button	2
	• Greet the customer and state your name	
	• Ask the customer's account number or other identifying information	
	• Access the customer's records	
Identify the purpose of the customer's call	• Ask the nature of the customer's request or complaint	4
	• Listen to the customer's information	
	• Ask follow-up questions to identify the purpose	
	• Paraphrase the customer's request or complaint	
Identify the appropriate solution	• List the options for the customer	4
	• Ask for the customer's reaction to the options	
	• Explain the option the customer prefers	
Gain agreement from the customer	• Ask the customer to agree	1
	• Record the option and assign a case number to the call	
Explain next steps	• Tell the customer how the preferred option will be implemented	2
	• Give the customer a case number	
	• Tell the customer how much time is needed to implement the preferred option	
End the call	• Thank the customer	3
	• Press a button to disconnect from the call	
	• Complete follow-up activity to implement the preferred option	

*for typical performer

Tool 7.1. Task Analysis Observation Template

Job:_____

Task:_____

Steps	Skills	Task difficulty* 1 = easy 5 = hard
1.		
2.		
3.		
4.		
5.		
6.		
7.		
8.		

*for typical performer

Training Needs Assessment. Copyright © 2006 by Jean Barbazette. Reproduced by permission of Pfeiffer, an Imprint of Wiley. www.pfeiffer.com

Figure 7.2. Sample Skill Hierarchy

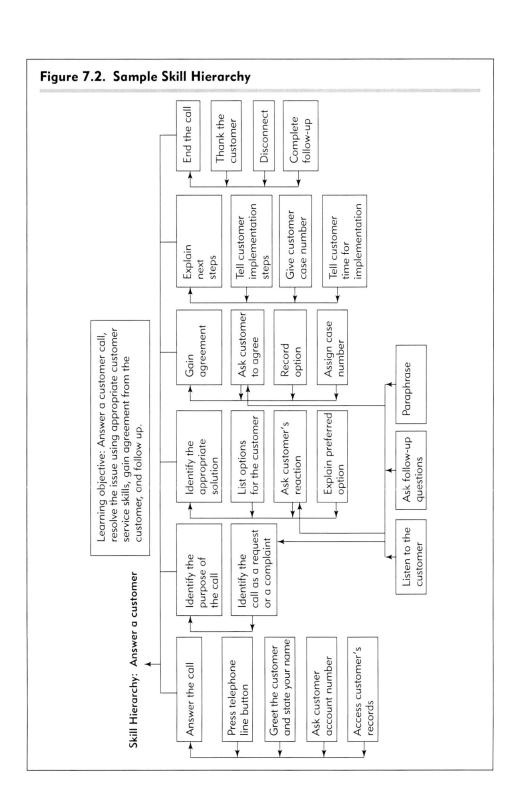

Skill Hierarchy: Answer a customer

Learning objective: Answer a customer call, resolve the issue using appropriate customer service skills, gain agreement from the customer, and follow up.

Answer the call
Press telephone line button
Greet the customer and state your name
Ask customer account number
Access customer's records

Identify the purpose of the call
Identify the call as a request or a complaint

Identify the appropriate solution
List options for the customer
Ask customer's reaction
Explain preferred option

Listen to the customer
Ask follow-up questions
Paraphrase

Gain agreement
Ask customer to agree
Record option
Assign case number

Explain next steps
Tell customer implementation steps
Give customer case number
Tell customer time for implementation

End the call
Thank the customer
Disconnect
Complete follow-up

A skill hierarchy is a graphic representation of the skills *any learner* must possess in order to meet the learning objective. It looks like an organization chart because it shows the *relationships* among skills. The hierarchy is not specific to a particular learner; it is specific to the task.

A skill hierarchy determines the sequence of learning the skills that is part of the new task and identifies prerequisites to learning to do the new task.

When creating a skill hierarchy from the top down, show the task written as a learning objective in the top level. In the second level, show what skills must be mastered before the learner can perform this task appropriately. Notice that the steps of the task are shown horizontally in the figure. The skills that enable a person to complete each step are shown below each step of the task. The third and lower levels show subskills (or subordinate skills). A subordinate skill must be learned before a superior skill. The arrows in the sample skill hierarchy show the subordinate relationship. Some subordinate skills apply to more than one step in the task, so use multiple arrows to show additional subordinate relationships.

Subordinate skills may contain skills that are prerequisites for the training session where this task is being taught. For example, accessing the customer's records and assigning case numbers are prerequisites taught in the customer software workshop and would not be part of this training session.

The next step in course development is to take the task analysis and skill hierarchy and write enabling learning objectives for the skills. When enabling objectives are achieved, the learning for the task is achieved. Following that, complete lesson plan development is needed. Lesson plan development will also be addressed in a later book in *The Skilled Trainer* series.

CHAPTER 8

TARGET POPULATION ANALYSIS

Chapter Objectives

- Describe who needs training using key characteristics
- Make decisions after target population analysis

Tools

- Decision Points List from Target Population Analysis

Chapter Questions

- What is the purpose of target population analysis?
- How is target population analysis conducted?
- What types of decisions are made from the results of a target population analysis?

What Is the Purpose of Target Population Analysis?

Target population analysis is used to collect information about who will attend the training. A target population analysis yields two types of information: first, it will help decide who needs training and how a specific course must be customized to meet the participants' needs, and second, it will identify what class groupings are appropriate. The results of a performance analysis can help identify who might need training. The results of a task analysis can tell who might need to be trained to complete a task in a standardized manner.

It might be that there are both primary and secondary target populations. In Chapter 4, the feasibility analysis example proposed training for retail store managers. It may be that assistant store managers would be an appropriate secondary analysis in this case.

How Is Target Population Analysis Conducted?

To conduct a target population analysis, collect information selected from the six categories below. Use at least three of the six categories to gather enough information to make appropriate customizing decisions. All six categories do not have equal importance for each training event. Decide what you want to find out about this particular group that can help you make content and enrollment or grouping decisions. Information is best collected from interviews, observations, or from existing information. Written surveys can raise unnecessary suspicions. For example, you may request information from customer service representatives about their attitudes toward training, their fluency in English, and what type of customer calls are the most difficult to handle well. Unless you explain why you want this type of information and what you will do with the results, you could get a defensive or suspicious reaction. Review existing records that are not confidential to provide an historical perspective.

Categories of Information[1]

1. *Interests:* What avocations, personal or business interests or current events are important to the target population? This information can be used to customize examples and exercises which relate to what is already

[1]Category titles adapted from Robert F. Mager and Kenneth M. Beach, Jr., *Developing Vocational Instruction.* Atlanta, GA: Center for Effective Performance, © 1967.

known. For example, if the customer service representatives are mostly young women who have interests in fitness, nutrition, and fashions, then select examples and analogies in class activities that build on those interests, rather than using hunting and sports examples.

2. *Prior Training:* Don't bore someone with repeated information. Knowing prior training attended by the target population will assist in making grouping decisions, identifying prerequisite requirements, and other administrative decisions. If customer service representatives have received product knowledge training and basic communications training, build on that information when creating examples that teach listening to irate customers and asking them questions.

3. *Personal Benefit to Learning:* What does the trainee get from the class that can be identified as personal or professional rewards? Keys to motivation may influence opening exercises and the need to develop supervisory support and follow-up for this training program. What's the WIIFM (What's in it for me)? For example, if customer service representatives know that the intended training will increase customer satisfaction and company bonuses are tied to that type of survey result, their level of interest in the training will increase.

4. *Attitudes and Biases:* Attitudes and biases dramatically influence selection of content, grouping, and supervisory follow-up. Three types of attitudes or biases can make a difference in how to approach this group for this training:

   • What is the learner's attitude toward his or her *job*? Is work defined by the learners as something you get paid for, doing what one is trained to do, or is the larger purpose of an employee's work evident? For example, do customer service representatives see this job as the beginning of a career, or are they saving money to attend college?

   • What is the learner's attitude toward *learning in general?* Do they learn something new all the time, or did meaningful learning end with formal schooling?

   • What is the learner's attitude toward *this specific class?* Is it mandated by law or company dictate? Is the class's reputation favorable or unfavorable? For example, do customer service representatives believe this training is to answer an unusually high number of customer complaints? Is the training intended to "fix" a problem? How do the customer service representatives feel about that problem?

5. *Physical Characteristics:* If physical characteristics make any difference at all, the age, gender, and physical dexterity of the target population could influence content and the amount of practice required to learn a skill. For example, older or more physically slight learners in a cardiopulmonary resuscitation (CPR) workshop might require more practice time to learn CPR. The more homogeneous the group, the easier it becomes to streamline the content and process of instruction, or to identify exceptions that require accommodation. For example, if any of the customer service representatives have a hearing disability, training on telephone equipment for the hearing impaired needs to be included in the training.

6. *Cultural Characteristics:* Identify the reading level of all employees, including non-native-English-speaking learners. The content and amount of material covered may have to be altered to match the reading level required on the job. Also consider characteristics of the corporate culture and how that might influence customizing the content for this class for this group. For example, if a large number of non-native English speakers are part of the customer service representative population, adjusting the vocabulary used in handout materials is appropriate.

Once these categories of information are developed, write a narrative statement that describes the target population. Three sample target population statements follow:

Target Population Statement Examples
Scientific Presentation Seminar[2]

The target population is a group of research scientists who must make electronic presentations to upper management over the Internet to:

- Show the status of their research
- Request more resources
- Request more time

---

[2]Contributed by Adrienne Kirkeby, Training Clinic Senior Instructor.

For approximately 75 percent of the scientists, English is their second language. Many of them are difficult to understand. They have complex content that must be presented accurately, clearly, and simply to be successful.

In general these scientists are extremely dedicated to their work, often viewing what they do as a service to mankind. They are highly educated and embrace learning as long as they can respect the instructor and the materials—view them as experts.

Teller Training[3]

New tellers are often interested in becoming tellers as an interim job. They may be attending school or they may see the teller position as a first career step. Most are in their late teens or in their twenties. They are in large part a generation brought up on television. Approximately half of the tellers are immigrants from another country and English is their second language.

Almost 50 percent of the population have been tellers before at a different bank. Many others come from a retail position. Our position pays more than other banks and has better hours. Most tellers are anxious to finish the training as soon as possible and get on to the real job.

Answering the Customer's Call

One hundred twenty customer service representatives (CSRs) work in a telephone call center for a retailer that sells home furnishings in retail stores, on the Internet, and through catalog sales. The call center receives calls from 8:00 a.m. to 10:00 p.m. (Eastern time) seven days a week. Most training is currently held during work hours with groups of twenty-five attending training at a time. Seventy-five percent are between the ages of eighteen and twenty-five, mostly young women. Twenty-four percent are women over forty who are returning to the workforce after raising their children. Most are interested in nutrition, fitness, and fashion and have brand loyalty to the products their company sells. Eighty percent have been on the job for at least one year and have attended training classes in product knowledge, ordering software, communication skills, and dealing with difficult customers. The other 20 percent have worked here for less than one year and only received ordering software and some product knowledge training.

---

[3]Contributed by Adrienne Kirkeby, Training Clinic Senior Instructor.

The CSRs are aware that the mandatory training will help resolve customer complaints more quickly. This will reduce the customer's wait time and perhaps improve the tone of interaction with an upset customer. Half of the eighteen-to-twenty-five-year-olds see their job as a way to make money to buy the things they enjoy. The other half sees a possible career ladder in the company. CSRs are somewhat relieved that the company is finally doing something to help them deal with the increasing number of angry customers. Two CSRs are slightly hearing impaired and wear hearing aids; but no accommodation is needed in how this class is delivered to the hearing impaired. Finally, 50 percent of the eighteen-to-twenty-five-year-olds are non-native English speakers. Spanish or Vietnamese is their native language.

What Types of Decisions Are Made from the Results of a Target Population Analysis?

In order to make several decisions, identify what additional information might be helpful and where this information might be found. Then consider making some of the decisions below. How these decisions are implemented might vary depending on how the training function is structured in different organizations. Many of the decisions suggested here might be made by a course developer or training manager, rather than by the needs assessor.

1. Remind the course developer who the typical learner is and suggest examples that might be appropriate for this group.

2. Identify the time constraints and how much practice is required to learn the skills and meet the course objectives for this training.

3. Identify how many people are included in this target population.

4. Identify how many groupings (basic, intermediate, advanced) will be needed to completely train this group.

5. Identify any prerequisites that need to be met for this training. Share these expectations and requirements with the supervisor of these employees.

6. Identify the need to create special examples or materials to meet the needs of subgroups of employees who will be trained.

7. Identify whether it is realistic to train all the employees in a specific group at the same time or using the same material. Decide whether it is

necessary to schedule part of the population to attend training while other employees keep the work going.

8. Suggest whether different levels of employees can be trained in the same group. Determine whether it is appropriate or threatening if supervisors are trained in the same group with their subordinates.

9. Identify how many supervisors and/or managers of the target population will need an overview or briefing to support the training effort.

10. To make the training as cost-effective as possible, identify any secondary target audience who can benefit from this training. Identify any additional cost to train this additional group. Identify the benefit to these employees and the organization to attend training that is not specifically targeted to them.

11. Identify the benefits of attending this training. Identify how this information and information about attitudes and biases for this training can be used to make appealing training announcements.

12. Identify any part of the target population who would not benefit from the training. For example, if a customer service representative is one month from retirement, she or he might be excused from attending the training. New employees who have yet to attend basic software and communications training might be scheduled for the last class offering so they have time to attend prerequisite training.

Tool 8.1 is a template that lists the twelve decisions.

Once these decisions are made, keep a written description with the course content materials. If the class is ongoing, review the written target population statement and decisions annually and adjust the statements for changes. Notify course developers and instructors of any needed changes as the target population changes. For example, if the retail call center were to expand its hours of operation, additional classes would be needed to accommodate the additional employees. Be sure that the new employees fit the profile developed from the existing target population. A more radical example would be for the call center to move its operation off shore. Then an entirely different statement would have to be researched and developed.

Many of the decisions made about the target population will build a foundation for contextual analysis, which is described in the next chapter.

Tool 8.1: Decision Points List from Target Population Analysis

Directions: Use this list to make decisions based on Target Population Analysis.

1. Are you aware of examples that are appropriate to train this group?

2. How much practice time is needed for this group?

3. How many people are in the total target population?

4. How many groups are needed to complete the training?

5. Identify prerequisites.

6. Do new examples need to be created for this group?

7. Can everyone be trained at the same time?

8. Can supervisors and their employees attend training together?

9. Is an overview needed for management?

10. Who is a secondary target population for this training?

11. What are the benefits of this training?

12. Who should be excluded from the training?

Training Needs Assessment. Copyright © 2006 by Jean Barbazette. Reproduced by permission of Pfeiffer, an Imprint of Wiley. www.pfeiffer.com

CHAPTER 9

CONTEXTUAL ANALYSIS

Chapter Objectives

- Create a plan to deliver training using different modes of delivery
- Identify how to schedule training events to avoid disrupting business
- Identify other requirements to deliver training

Tools

- Contextual Analysis Checklist

Chapter Questions

- What is contextual analysis?
- How will the training be delivered?
- When will the training be presented?
- What are the other requirements to deliver the training?

What Is Contextual Analysis?

Contextual analysis takes information from other analyses described in earlier chapters and answers how, when, and where training will be delivered. It helps you compare different delivery mediums and address scheduling issues and other logistics within the context of the organization and the learning objectives.

How Will the Training Be Delivered?

Once the target population and the learning objectives are identified, select the best medium or setting to deliver training to reach those objectives. Training can be delivered to a group of learners, one individual, self-paced, or on the job. For example, the learning objectives in interpersonal or supervisory skills training often involve practice with other participants to achieve mastery. Group training in a physical classroom seems more appropriate than self-paced training delivered over the Internet.

Delivery Options by Class Size

Group training can be delivered in a physical or virtual classroom. *Individual or self-paced* training can be delivered using a variety of high-tech (computer-based training) and low-tech options (complete a workbook) in a physical or virtual classroom described in greater detail below. *On-the-job* training is usually delivered in the workplace and is delivered to one learner or a small group of learners.

Figure 9.1 shows items to compare when choosing how training will be delivered using five factors: cost, consistency, timely delivery, expertise of the trainer, and other considerations. Delivery *cost* is highest among the three options for on-the-job training, since the time of the trainer or supervisor is repeated each time one person or a small group is trained.

Consistency can be maintained best when the entire group hears the same message and experiences the same training together. The more often training is repeated, the greater the opportunity for a variety of messages to be heard. In self-paced training, consistency depends on the quality of the materials.

Delivery time looks at how many people can be trained within a short period of time. If two hundred people are trained in one group or eight smaller groups, the training can be accomplished quickly. Conversely, if two hundred employees are required to take self-paced training by themselves, there are likely to be compliance issues. It will take the longest time to train two hundred employees individually or in small groups.

Expertise of the trainer must be high when the content expert meets with the group. The expertise of the trainer for self-paced training must be imbedded in the materials, since the individual reading the self-paced material usually does not have the opportunity to clarify understanding with the trainer. Expertise of the trainer for on-the-job delivery is rated medium, since most OJT trainers have subject-matter expertise, but little adult learning knowledge and skill.

Other considerations beyond the actual delivery of training include added travel costs if the target population needs to travel to join the group session. Self-paced training experiences a larger dropout rate than classroom training. Learners must have internal motivation to finish a self-paced course. If choosing to deliver training on-the-job, real materials are consumed and regular production work is delayed while training occurs.

Figure 9.1. Comparison of Delivery Options by Class Size

Delivery Option	Cost	Consistency	Delivery Time	Required Expertise of Trainer	Other Considerations
Group	Medium	High	Low	High	Travel costs
Self-paced	Medium	Medium	Medium	High	Dropout rate
On the job	High	Low	High	Medium	Waste and delay

Physical and Virtual Delivery Options

To decide whether a physical or virtual classroom is most appropriate, consider the physical location of the target population and whether the time away from the job to travel is excessive or more expensive than the virtual classroom option. For example, a synchronous (learners attend training at the same time, not necessarily in the same place) four-hour workshop was conducted in a U.S. federal government agency via satellite for over two hundred employees at eighty downlinks. This choice was more cost-effective than paying travel expenses for two hundred employees to reach the same location. Figure 9.2 shows a comparison of two delivery options, virtual and physical.

When comparing *location cost,* once a physical classroom is built, the only cost is the cost per square foot to use and maintain that space. Once a learning management system is purchased, the only cost is to use and maintain the system.

Travel costs for a widely disbursed population can be high for the physical classroom delivery option. However, if the target population is not widely disbursed,
travel cost is not a factor when comparing physical and virtual classrooms.

Timely delivery of training depends on the availability of the physical classroom. The more training programs presented at a given facility, the greater the
competition for that space. It is often easier to schedule virtual training than
physical space.

The requirement for trainer expertise is often higher when the trainer can physically see the participants. The virtual trainer must actively work to overcome
the barrier of loss of sight to be effective.

Distractions can plague both the physical and virtual classroom. In the physical classroom, disruptive participants can start side conversations, enter and
leave the classroom, use cell phones and all manner of other distractions. In the
virtual classroom, the greatest distraction is multi-tasking by bored participants
or dropping out prior to the conclusion of training.

Figure 9.2. Comparison Between Physical and Virtual Delivery Options

Delivery Option	Location Cost	Travel Cost for Widely Disbursed Population	Schedule Timely Delivery	Required Expertise of Trainer	Other Considerations
Physical	Medium	High	Medium ease	High	Distractions or disruptions
Virtual	Medium	Low	High ease	Medium	Dropout rate

Delivery Options by Location

If group training is conducted in a physical classroom, decide whether the
space available at the organization's location is appropriate for use as a classroom. Other physical classroom locations might include rented space at a hotel,
conference center, or learning laboratory. Some workshops, such as strategic
planning and team building, are best held offsite to avoid interruptions and
distractions of corporate classrooms. Figure 9.3 compares factors when conducting training onsite and offsite.

The *cost* of using existing training space is lower compared to a hotel or conference center. *The ease of scheduling* an internal facility is simpler, when compared to external facilities, where competition for space can be greater. However,
if there is great competition for internal space, these ratings would change.

Generally, the *quality of catered food and service* increases when using higher-end facilities like conference centers. Obviously, there are exceptions to this statement. *Other considerations* for selecting a training site include fewer interruptions of participants at an external site. Weigh that against the travel time for participants to reach the external site. Often at conference centers and resort properties, sports, shopping, and other interests compete with attending training.

Figure 9.3. Comparison of Delivery Options by Location

Delivery Option	Location Cost	Ease of Scheduling	Quality of Food and Service	Other Considerations
Onsite	Low	Variable	Variable	Interruptions
Offsite hotel	Medium	Medium	Medium	Travel time
Offsite conference center	High	Variable	High	Competing interests Travel time

Five Virtual Delivery Options

Virtual classroom options include synchronous training delivered via satellite, video and/or telephone conferencing, the Internet, or intranet via a local area network (LAN). The software program delivered over the LAN is called a learning management system (LMS). Resources that discuss how to select an LMS are listed in the Bibliography.

Asynchronous training (learners attend training alone at different times) is self-paced training delivered via the Internet, CD or DVD, or local area network. Also, asynchronous training can be attended by a group of individuals who learn the same material at different times. How asynchronous training is delivered often depends on the resources available in a given organization. For example, consider whether the target population has access to a computer with a DVD drive or Internet access with a high-speed connection. If the training has streaming video or complex graphics as part of the session, delivery will be more troublefree using a DVD or a high-speed connection, not a dial-up modem. If the target population is attending training in a virtual classroom that uses the Internet, consult with your organization's information technology department about firewall and other access issues.

Figure 9.4 compares virtual delivery options for training. The initial *cost of purchase* shows that the more sophisticated the technology, the higher the cost.

Again, the *cost of delivery* for an individual training event decreases with the sophistication of the technology.

The *consistency* of the training content is high in all delivery mediums for the virtual classroom. Everyone sees the same message. The *timeliness of delivery* depends on the availability of the technology and the schedules of the individuals who are to attend the training. Looking at the availability of the technology alone, it usually takes longer to schedule satellite delivery than video or telephone conferencing. Intranet and CD or DVD delivery is controlled internally, so it is usually easier to schedule delivery. Internet-delivered training often depends on an external provider and is subject to their schedule as well as internal schedules. As for the *expertise of the trainer,* the synchronous delivery methods depend on the content and technical expertise of the trainer. The more a skilled physical classroom trainer practices with the virtual delivery medium, the greater the transference of the trainer's skills from the physical to the virtual classroom. Even the most expert physical classroom trainer requires technical help in getting the most from the virtual delivery medium. With the CD or DVD option, direct communication with the trainer is a greater challenge.

Finally, optimum *class size* for each virtual delivery option is only limited by the technology. Including more than five video or telephone conference sites makes participation difficult.

Figure 9.4. Comparison of Five Virtual Delivery Options

Delivery Option for Virtual Classroom	Cost of Purchase	Cost of Delivery	Consistency	Timely Delivery	Required Expertise of Trainer	Class Size
Satellite	High	High	High	Medium	Medium	Virtually unlimited
Video conference	Medium	Medium	High	High	Medium	Best used with fewer than five sites
Intranet (LMS)	High	Medium	High	High	Medium	Virtually unlimited
Internet	High	Medium	High	Medium	Medium	Virtually unlimited
CD or DVD	Low	Low	High	High	Low	Individual

Finally, consider whether a *blended* learning option is appropriate to meet the learning objectives. Blended learning delivery options include attending training using more than one delivery medium. For example, interpersonal skills like mentoring can be taught by starting with a self-paced component to read background information about essential elements of mentoring programs or to complete a personal assessment (either hard copy or online).

Next, a group discussion around mentoring issues/problems can be conducted in a physical classroom or synchronous session using the Internet. The target population can complete specific assignments to begin mentoring a protégé and report back to the group at the next meeting.

After deciding on the medium to deliver training, consider when to schedule the training.

When Will the Training Be Presented?

To schedule a training session, first consider the size of the target population and whether attendance is mandatory or voluntary. Decide whether a specific training session is a part of several sessions, or independent of other training. Can individual sessions of a series be taken in random or sequential order?

What is the availability of skilled trainers to present the training? Are trainers internal employees or external contract trainers? What is the optimum size group to meet the learning objective and not exceed the physical space available? For example, an information briefing or update is easily conducted for a large number of learners. However, if skill development is part of the objective, practice and feedback are needed to develop a skill and a class size of twelve to twenty will bring better learning results.

Finally, consider other restrictions that can impact training. Many organizations do not conduct voluntary training on Monday or Friday, since other work-related and personal-related issues compete for the learners' attention on those days. Often the beginning or end of a month is a difficult time to conduct training due to business needs and reporting requirements. Holidays and peak vacation times should be avoided.

Decide whether training is to be conducted during work hours and employees are released from regular work to attend training. Some organizations conduct training before or after normal work hours and compensate employees by paying overtime or providing equivalent time off. Discuss workload considerations with supervisors to determine how many employees can be away from work to attend training as a group. Sometimes it is difficult for employees to be away from work for more than a few hours, so a one-day workshop might need to be scheduled as two half-day sessions, or even four two-hour sessions. If employees must be replaced while attending training, the availability of replacement personnel must be considered.

What Are the Other Requirements to Deliver the Training?

Some training requires that employees complete pre-work prior to attending. Consider how this requirement can be met by the employees attending training. Will employees be given time away from their regular duties to complete pre-work, or are they to complete pre-work on their own time?

Some training requires practice in between sessions. When and where will employees complete these practice sessions or homework assignments? If practice sessions include applying what is learned in the classroom to the job, what tools are provided for the practice? How will the employee's supervisor be involved in practice sessions? Will the learner use a checklist or skills observation sheet to report practice and progress between class sessions?

Consider whether there are other requirements to deliver training. For example, if employees are union workers, some provisions in the labor contract might affect training.

What type of record-keeping for attendance at training is required?

Be sure to consider these and other requirements when scheduling training sessions.

Let's revisit the "Customer Call Training" for the 120 customer service representatives described in Chapters 6 through 8 and identify how training would be delivered for this workshop. Half of the 120 CSRs work from 7:00 a.m. to 3:00 p.m. and the other half work from 3:00 p.m. to 11:00 p.m. The learning objectives for this training include practice to develop interpersonal skills through discussions and role plays. Since all 120 employees work in the same place, group training in a physical (not virtual) classroom is most cost-effective and addresses the learning objectives for this mandatory training.

Supervisors request that the training be delivered in two four-hour modules with no more than twenty CSRs attending training at a time. No training for this group is held on Mondays, since that is a peak call day. Conducting training before or after a shift would incur overtime expenses that the company was not willing to pay. Therefore, schedule six classes of twenty people each (three for the first shift and three for the second shift) for the first module and another six classes for the second module of training. This organization has two classrooms that are shared with other departments that conduct training. The schedule for the next two months shows one classroom is available on each shift every Friday. For consistency, only two trainers will teach all the classes. One trainer is assigned to the first shift, and the other trainer is assigned to the second shift. The supervisors and the trainers will listen to live calls between the presentations of the modules to find out whether what was learned in the classroom transferred to the job.

The checklist in Tool 9.1 can remind you of all the contextual requirements to consider. Contextual analysis is the last type of analysis explained in this book. Look at the final chapter to learn how to summarize all the data from all the analyses into a training plan for presentation to management.

Tool 9.1. Contextual Analysis Checklist

How will training be delivered?

- ❑ Group
- ❑ Individual or self-paced
- ❑ On the job

Where will training be delivered?

- ❑ Physical classroom
  - ❑ Organization's site
  - ❑ Off-site at conference center, hotel, or learning laboratory
- ❑ Virtual classroom
  - ❑ Synchronous training (same time, not necessarily same place)
    - ❑ Satellite down-link
    - ❑ Video conference
    - ❑ Telephone conference

Training Needs Assessment. Copyright © 2006 by Jean Barbazette. Reproduced by permission of Pfeiffer, an Imprint of Wiley. www.pfeiffer.com

Tool 9.1. Contextual Analysis Checklist, Cont'd

- ❑ Asynchronous training (learners attend at different time, different place)
  - ❑ Internet
  - ❑ CD or DVD
  - ❑ Local area network
  - ❑ Video
  - ❑ Printed workbook
- ❑ On the job
- ❑ Blended options

When will training be presented?
Consider these requirements or restrictions:

- ❑ Days of the week
- ❑ Workload
- ❑ Peak times during the month
- ❑ Organization holidays
- ❑ Peak vacation or leave times
- ❑ Space available
- ❑ Optimum size of the group
- ❑ Training during work hours or before or after work hours
- ❑ Number of hours permitted away from the job
- ❑ Compliance with collective bargaining agreement
- ❑ Pre-work options
- ❑ Practice required in between workshop sessions
- ❑ Record-keeping of attendance at training sessions

Training Needs Assessment. Copyright © 2006 by Jean Barbazette. Reproduced by permission of Pfeiffer, an Imprint of Wiley. www.pfeiffer.com

CHAPTER 10

DEVELOP AND PRESENT A TRAINING PLAN TO MANAGEMENT

Chapter Objectives

- Learn how to complete a ten-part training plan
- Identify competencies to develop a training plan
- Learn how to present a training plan to management and gain approval

Tools

- Training Plan Template

Chapter Questions

- What is in a ten-part training plan?
- How is a plan presented to management to gain approval?

What Is in a Ten-Part Training Plan?

Following the completion of one or more needs analyses, a training plan is usually written to report the results of the analyses and to meet projected training needs for a group of employees (for example, first-line supervisors, customer service representatives) or for a period of time, such as for the coming year. Here are the ten parts of a training plan, along with references to which type of analysis would develop each type of information. To get buy-in from management, link the outcome or symptom from each analysis to a business need.

1. Issue Definition

Define the issues that are related to a business need that training can address. For example, for either of the following issues it would be appropriate to develop a training plan:

- How can we successfully open ten new stores with the current skills of the assistant store managers who would be promoted to store manager?

- Middle managers have no advanced training beyond what they received when they became supervisors.

Often the issues are identified by completing a *performance analysis*. Remember to offer non-training recommendations where appropriate.

2. Need Identification (vs. Wants)

Some organizations get trapped into putting on training programs because they are popular or requested, without regard for linking training to a business need. Often a request for time management, stress management, or communication skills indicates "needs" that ought to be sorted out from "wants." Identify how widespread the "need" or "want" is and whether or not it is related to job performance. A *needs versus wants analysis* develops this type of information.

3. Contract with Supervisors

How will supervisors or managers of those attending training be included in the planning and follow-up for improved performance? Define the role of the supervisor or manager of the participants and identify how to prepare them to support, enable, and reinforce the training.

4. Identify/Establish Performance Standards

Often training is requested to improve performance. Is there a performance standard to use as the goal for a minimum level of acceptable performance? The operational area, not training, has to establish job performance standards. It becomes difficult to train if vague or no standards exist. ("Just make them more professional" is an example of a request that may or may not have an agreed-on standard of acceptable job performance.)

Information related to performance standards is developed *from job/task analysis, performance analysis*, and *goal analysis.*

5. Trainee Identification

Who is to be trained? What job classifications do they hold and how many people need training? *Target population analysis* develops this type of information.

6. Establish Training Objectives and Training Evaluation Criteria and Results

Identify how you will know the training is successful. How will learning and new skills be evaluated? How will you tie training to bottom-line results and back to the business need that dictates the training?

This information is developed by conducting a *performance analysis* and *needs versus wants analysis.*

7. Cost of Training

What are the costs to assess the need for training, design the training, develop learner and instructor materials, and present the training and evaluate the training? Are the costs worth the benefit?

A *feasibility analysis* develops this type of information.

8. Select/Develop the Training Program

Decide whether you will present an existing program or buy a packaged training program. Decide whether you will use internal subject-matter experts as developers/trainers or hire an external consultant, designer, or trainer.

No needs analysis tool is used to answer this question completely. Perhaps a *contextual analysis* can answer some of the issues around program selection.

9. Scheduling

What time of the day, week, month, quarter, or year is best for this type of training? What are the consequences of training "on the clock" or on the employee's own time in your organization?

Contextual analysis develops this type of information.

10. Evaluate the Results

Apply the criteria using these four levels and objectives from number 6 above.

- Participant reaction
- Learning
- Job performance
- Results

Exhibit 10.1 is an example of a training plan to conduct training for department managers for a hotel chain in the United States.

Exhibit 10.1. Sample Training Plan

Department Managers' Training
Purpose (Issue Definition and Outcome)

The purpose of this plan is to describe the need for a Department Manager Training Program and to describe how that can be accomplished. Department Managers have received basic supervisory training through a commercial self-paced, video-based program. Approximately 30 percent of all Department Managers completed one or more modules of the self-paced program. The new Department Manager Training Program would supplement the basic program and be presented over four and a half days.

Managers are facing tasks and responsibilities for which they have received no training. Some department managers are experiencing higher than normal turnover, and a few grievances have been filed for perceived unfair employee treatment. The training will include conducting performance planning and reviews for their supervisory reports as well as build

Exhibit 10.1. Sample Training Plan, Cont'd

supervisory retention. Many managers have been promoted from the position of supervisor and require planning, organizing, and coaching skills, which are different skills used in the "hands-on" supervision position they used to hold. The issues are described in each of the eight suggested topics that were developed from extensive interviews with department heads and their managers.

This need is not unique, and existing unused materials were developed by different authors in different formats over a period of time. A standard format and lesson plan has to be developed by either internal or external sources into an eight-unit Department Manager Training Program from the existing materials.

Department Heads (Performance Standards and Target Population)

All department heads would be included in the training. This also includes anyone who has supervisors reporting to him or her. This includes approximately 250 managers throughout the company in a dozen locations. Managers of departments have been interviewed and asked to make standards of performance for Department Managers more objective and fair. Department Managers' performance would be evaluated during a performance planning and review session as outlined in the new "Quality Service Program" that has just been completed.

Deliverables (Training Criteria)

The products to be developed for this eight-unit training program would include:

1. Participant handout materials in a uniform format.

2. Leaders' guides for each unit in a uniform format.

3. An application tool from each unit to assist the department manager in the use of the information learned. This would give the manager an additional tool for evaluation and use of new skills on the job.

Exhibit 10.1. Sample Training Plan, Cont'd

Eight Units of Content

1. Basics of Management	four hours
2. Employee Selection	four hours
3. Training and Development	four hours
4. Performance Planning	three hours
5. Performance Appraisal	three hours
6. Labor Relations	eight hours
7. Coaching	two hours
8. Stress Management	four hours

Cost of Training

The time to develop each module in a consistent format from existing materials is an average of six days for an experienced training department course designer.

There is additional time for one to two days of coaching for instructors by the course developer(s) and one week for the pilot and two days for revisions.

The total cost of the project will range from $9,000 to $10,000, depending on the salary and benefits package of the training department employees selected to do the job. Costs on a per person basis will be charged back to those who attend the training.

Schedule

Phase I: Design and Development
The Training Department is prepared to begin work within one week of the acceptance of this plan. As each module is completed, it will be submitted to management for review and approval.

Exhibit 10.1. Sample Training Plan, Cont'd

If the plan is accepted by July 17, the following schedule is an example of what could be accomplished:

Unit 1	July 24
Unit 2	July 31
Unit 3	August 7
Unit 4	August 14
Unit 5	August 21
Unit 6	August 28
Unit 7	September 5
Unit 8	September 11
Coaching	September 18
Pilot	September 25–29
Revisions	October 1–5

Phase II: Training

Two trainers would be available to present the workshop between October 10 and December 10. Twenty Department Heads could be trained at the twelve locations over a six-week schedule. A make-up class will be scheduled in a central location for those unable to attend the workshop held at their location during the last week of January.

Role of Managers (Partnership with Management)

Managers and Directors to whom the Department Managers report will meet with the Department Manager before and after training to discuss specific goals and objectives for each Department Manager as they relate to his or her job tasks. Managers and Directors will be given an overview of the week-long workshop and copies of the tools and action plans used

---

Exhibit 10.1. Sample Training Plan, Cont'd

during training. Suggestions to tie new skills to the Department Manager's performance planning and review process will also be provided. Managers and Directors will be asked to provide coverage during the week that a Department Manager attends training.

Evaluation Criteria

Level 1: The Department Heads will be asked to identify how the training met their needs through an end-of-course evaluation for each of the eight units of content.

Level 2: Through a pre-test (which really looks like a survey, rather than a test) prior knowledge is gathered in an assessment process. Post-test evaluation takes place during the course as knowledge is demonstrated in discussions and skill performance is demonstrated through class exercises.

Level 3: Each Department Manager completes an action plan that is shared back on the job with the Director to whom the Department Manager reports. Monthly checks are made against the action plans. Performance Planning and review sessions are ongoing.

Level 4: Performance indicators are collected prior to the training that would be impacted by the training, such as department turnover, complaint data from customer surveys, number of sick days, number of grievances, accident rates, and other measures. Additional measures are taken on a monthly basis.

A training plan template is given in Tool 10.1.

Tool 10.1. Training Plan Template

_____ 1. Issue defined clearly.

_____ 2. Reaffirm the outcome, results, or objectives of the plan.

_____ 3. Clearly state the performance deficiency and its causes.

_____ 4. Identify/establish performance standards.

_____ 5. Identify target population.

_____ 6. Establish evaluation criteria.

_____ 7. Describe proposed intervention.

_____ 8. Estimate the cost of the plan.

_____ 9. Build a partnership with management.

_____ 10. Schedule according to business demands.

_____

Training Needs Assessment. Copyright © 2006 by Jean Barbazette. Reproduced by permission of Pfeiffer, an Imprint of Wiley. www.pfeiffer.com

How Is a Plan Presented to Management to Gain Approval?

How a training plan is presented to management (or the client) to gain approval depends on the decision-making process in each organization. If the internal client who requested a training plan or some type of needs assessment is the management decision maker, ask the client what type of information he or she needs to make a decision. What amount of discussion and detail is sought? Does the client prefer to see a summary of data or both a summary and raw data from which the summary is drawn? Does the client prefer to make decisions from the data or to select from recommendations made by the trainer conducting the needs analyses?

Since most training plans are complex, it is helpful to provide a one-page overview and allow time to read the plan prior to discussing it. Provide a copy of the plan to managers at least a week before meeting to discuss the plan along with a proposed agenda or questions for discussion. Most plans need some additional explanation and discussion before budgetary approval is given. Exhibit 10.2 is a sample agenda for a meeting where a training plan is presented to management.

Often presenting parts of the training plan visually can help clarify what is or is not a part of the training plan.

Exhibit 10.2. Sample Training Plan Presentation Agenda

1. Confirmation of the business need and reason for the needs assessment.

2. Description of the types of needs analyses conducted and summary of data collected.

3. Questions for our discussion:

   • Based on a prior needs assessment, to what extent will the current eight topics meet the needs of department managers? What events might explain a request for stress management by this group? What other issues or events are we trying to address through training on these topics?

   • Is the cost of training and the time involved for department managers worth the potential benefits?

   • Is the fourth-quarter schedule reasonable given the time of year for the department managers to attend training for four consecutive days? Should training be conducted in the first quarter of the following year?

   • How can we increase the support of directors and senior managers for this initiative?

   • Is the organization willing to commit to measuring performance indicators that demonstrate return on this investment of training?

   • What is the current number of department managers who would be involved in training?

4. Make decisions on training recommendations. Review non-training recommendations and make decisions.

Various templates used in Chapters 2 through 9 are presented on the CD-ROM accompanying this book.

Next Steps

The presentation of a training plan is both an ending of one process and the beginning of another. Once decisions are made from the training plan, identify who will follow up on those decisions. How will this information be handed off to the course developer? How will management inform the target population of the training and non-training solutions selected to address the performance issues? Who will coordinate and implement the decisions made from the training plan?

Future books in *The Skilled Trainer* series will address course design and development, appropriate use of different training methods, and techniques to measure the results of training.

What Are the Competencies for Needs Assessments?

Trainers and course designers are responsible for assessing training needs and designing training programs and developing a training plan to meet the organization's needs. Competencies required for an effective needs assessor include identifying what type of information is required and knowing how to collect it and analyze it efficiently, along with shaping a training plan based on the information collected. Competencies for needs assessment and developing a training plan follow.

Needs Assessor and Training Plan Competency Checklists

Following are two checklists that define the needs assessment competencies and training plan competencies for the trainer or course designer to assess training needs. Together they become a competency model for the needs assessor.

All the competencies describe the optimum behaviors for the needs assessor. When reviewing competencies for a needs assessor, identify whether the needs assessor does the tasks described. Ratings of "A" and "B" distinguish whether the competency is held at the "advanced" or "basic" level. For either an "A" or "B" rating, tangible results or output are visible. A rating of "I" stands for "incomplete" because tangible results or output are not observed, are missing, or are partially complete. Remember that competency is either observed or is not observed.

Following the Needs Assessor and Training Plan Competency Model Checklist is a second set of checklists. The first of these expands on the numbered needs assessor competencies and provides a description of the *basic* competency along

---

[1]The material in this section is largely taken from the first book in this series by Jean Barbazette: *The Trainer's Journey to Competence.* San Francisco: Pfeiffer. Used with permission.

with supporting knowledge, skills, and attitudes. Results or output for each competency are also provided. Another checklist is provided with *advanced* competency descriptions with supporting knowledge, skills, and attitudes. At the end of the Needs Assessor Competency Model Checklist, the rater shows the total percentage of competencies observed. Remember to decide prior to the observation what percentage of competencies must be present to show competence.

Uses for the Competency Checklists

Use competency checklists to rate yourself or as part of a collaborative process when being rated by another person. To customize the needs assessor competency model, first review the checklists. Next, select those competencies that are either required or desirable for the needs assessor role in your organization. Download the desired checklists from the CD that accompanies the first book in the series to create a customized checklist. Either eliminate the competencies that do not apply or rate the competency as N/A for "not applicable." Prior to assessing a competency, agree with the rater on the meaning of the competencies. Review the expanded descriptions with supporting knowledge, skills, and attitudes to determine *basic* versus *advanced* levels of competency. Also, when rating another person, ensure a shared definition of each competency and what level of competency is being assessed.

Competency Model Checklist for Course Designers

A = meets *advanced* competency (advanced tangible results or outputs are visible)

B = meets *basic* competency (tangible results or outputs are visible)

I = *incomplete* (tangible results or outputs are not observed, missing or partially complete)

N = behavior *not* observed (not competent)

Rating	Course Designer Competency	Basic Results or Output	Advanced Results or Output
Planning Competencies: Needs Assessment			
	1. Uses performance analysis to sort training and non-training issues	Training recommendations	Performance analysis report
	2. Uses target population analysis to identify critical elements about the intended participants.	Target population statement Recommendations	Target population statement Recommendations
	3. Conducts a "needs versus wants" analysis to identify common needs of a specific target population.	Data summary Recommendations	Data summary Recommendations
	4. Conducts a job analysis to identify critical job success elements	Data summary Recommendations	Data summary Recommendations
	5. Conducts a task analysis to break a task into its teachable parts.	Task breakdown	Task breakdown
	6. Creates a skill hierarchy to identify supporting skills and course prerequisites	Skill hierarchy Course prerequisites	Skill hierarchy Course prerequisites
Planning Competencies: Training Plan			
	7. Identifies the training issue and how it relates to a business need	Training plan to justify a training event request	Training plan issues related to a business need
	8. States the outcome, results, and objectives of the training	Training event rationale	Training plan results
	9. States the performance deficiency and its causes	Training event justification	Performance deficiencies and causes
	10. Identifies or establishes performance standards	Performance standards	Performance standards
	11. Identifies the target population	Target population statement	Target population statement

Competency Model Checklist for Course Designers, Cont'd

Rating	Course Designer Competency	Basic Results or Output	Advanced Results or Output
	12. Establishes criteria to evaluate the training	Evaluation tools	Evaluation tools
	13. Describes the proposed intervention	Training event description	Variety of activities and interventions
			Job aids
	14. Estimates the cost of the training plan	Estimated costs	Feasibility cost estimate
	15. Builds a partnership with management to ensure success of the training plan	Training announcement	Partnership roles
	16. Schedules training	Training schedule	Training schedule

Competencies for Needs Assessors

Basic Needs Assessment Competency 1: Uses Performance Analysis to Sort Training and Non-Training Issues

Asks questions to identify which issues are training needs and which are non-training needs. Recommends training solutions where appropriate.

Results or Output

Training recommendations

Supporting Knowledge

- Understands what type of questions are appropriate
- Is aware of appropriate people to interview

Supporting Skills

- Asks appropriate questions
- Distinguishes between training and non-training issues
- Makes recommendations for training issues

Supporting Attitudes

- Is willing to have developed data determine the outcome and recommendations

Advanced Needs Assessment Competency 1: Uses Performance Analysis to Sort Training and Non-Training Issues

Conducts a performance analysis to identify which issues are training needs and which are non-training needs. Recommends training solutions where appropriate.

Results or Output

Performance analysis report

Supporting Knowledge

- Understands informal and formal methodologies to conduct a performance analysis
- Understands what type of questions are appropriate
- Is aware of appropriate people to interview
- Understands survey techniques to collect and interpret statistically significant data

Supporting Skills

- Uses informal and formal performance analysis tools appropriately
- Asks appropriate questions
- Distinguishes between training and non-training issues
- Makes recommendations for training issues
- Ties training recommendations to business needs

Supporting Attitudes

- Is willing to have developed data determine the outcome and recommendations
- Is interested in conserving resources for true training needs
- Is interested in the deeper or root causes of issues or problems

Basic Needs Assessment Competency 2: Uses Target Population Analysis to Identify Critical Elements About the Intended Participants

Identifies information to make appropriate content and grouping decisions.

Results or Output

Target population statement, recommendations

Supporting Knowledge

- Is aware of which people or employees constitute the target population
- Is aware of information to seek about the target population
- Understands the decisions that will be made based on the data collected

Supporting Skills

- Asks appropriate questions
- Interviews a sufficient number of the target population to make appropriate recommendations
- Writes justifications for content selection and grouping decisions based on the data

Supporting Attitude

- Shows sensitivity to the needs of the target population

Advanced Needs Assessment Competency 2: Uses Target Population Analysis to Identify Critical Elements About the Intended Participants

Identifies information in six critical areas to make appropriate content and grouping decisions.

Results or Output

Target population statement, recommendations

Supporting Knowledge

- Is aware of which people or employees constitute the target population
- Is aware of different types of information to seek about the target population
- Understands the decisions that will be made based on the data collected
- Understands what constitutes appropriate questions for a specific target population
- Understands survey techniques to collect and interpret statistically significant data

Supporting Skills

- Asks appropriate questions
- Interviews a sufficient number of the target population to make appropriate recommendations
- Collects information through surveys when appropriate
- Writes justifications for content selection and grouping decisions based on the data and the business needs

Supporting Attitudes

- Is sensitive to the needs of the target population
- Avoids making the target population defensive and unwilling to answer questions

Basic Needs Assessment Competency 3: Conducts a "Needs Versus Wants" Analysis to Identify Common Needs of a Specific Target Population

Creates a list of desired skills the target population may need or want and surveys the population to identify common needs.

Results or Output

Data summary, recommendations

Supporting Knowledge

- Is aware of whom to survey
- Is aware of which types of content topics to list in a survey

Supporting Skills

- Creates a survey of training topics
- Collects and summarizes survey data
- Makes recommendations on which courses would be appropriate from the data

Supporting Attitudes

- Is open-minded
- Shows flexibility in making interpretations from the data

Advanced Needs Assessment Competency 3: Conducts a "Needs Versus Wants" Analysis to Identify Common Needs of a Specific Target Population

Identifies a list of desired skills the target population may need or want and surveys the population to identify common needs. Identifies which managers and subordinates of the target population might be surveyed to gain additional perspectives of the target population's training needs.

Results or Output

Data summary, recommendations

Supporting Knowledge

- Is aware of whom to survey
- Is aware of which types of content topics to list in a survey
- Is aware of survey techniques to create valid recommendations
- Understands survey techniques to collect and interpret statistically significant data

Supporting Skills

- Creates an appropriate survey that can be taken online
- Collects and synthesizes data
- Conducts a feedback meeting with the client sponsors and/or managers to help interpret data
- Makes recommendations on which courses would be appropriate from the data and based on business needs

Supporting Attitudes

- Is open-minded
- Is flexible in making interpretations from the data
- Is interested in the deeper or root causes of issues or problems

Basic Needs Assessment Competency 4: Conducts a Job Analysis to Identify Critical Job Success Elements

With assistance from subject-matter experts, analyzes job elements to identify critical tasks required to perform a job successfully.

Results or Output

Data summary, recommendations

Supporting Knowledge

- Is aware of job elements
- Is aware of what makes a task critical
- Understands interviewing and questioning skills

Supporting Skills

- Asks questions of subject-matter experts to identify critical tasks in a job
- Summarizes data
- Makes course content recommendations

Supporting Attitude

- Is interested in creating a thorough and accurate report

Advanced Competency 4: Conducts a Job Analysis to Identify Critical Job Success Elements

Analyzes job elements to identify critical tasks required to perform a job successfully.

Results or Output

Data summary, recommendations

Supporting Knowledge

- Is aware of job elements
- Understands what makes a task critical
- Understands hierarchies
- Understands interviewing and questioning skills

Supporting Skills

- Asks basic and follow-up questions of subject-matter experts to identify critical tasks in a job
- Summarizes data
- Makes course content recommendations based on data and business needs

Supporting Attitude

- Is interested in creating a thorough and accurate report

Basic Needs Assessment Competency 5: Conducts a Task Analysis to Break a Task into Its Teachable Parts

With the help of subject-matter experts, analyzes task elements to identify critical steps required to perform a task successfully.

Results or Output

Task breakdown

Supporting Knowledge

- Is aware of job elements
- Is aware of what makes a task critical
- Understands interviewing and questioning skills
- Understands how to complete a task observation and documentation

Supporting Skills

- Lists the critical steps in performing a specific task
- Asks a subject-matter expert to estimate the difficulty of doing the task by a typical performer
- Observes and interviews a master performer doing the task
- Validates documentation by making a final observation

Supporting Attitude

- Is interested in being accurate and complete in documentation

Advanced Needs Assessment Competency 5: Conducts a Task Analysis to Break a Task into Its Teachable Parts

Analyzes task elements to identify critical steps required to perform a task successfully.

Results or Output

Task breakdown

Supporting Knowledge

- Is aware of job elements
- Understands what makes a task critical
- Understands hierarchies
- Understands interviewing and questioning skills
- Understands how to complete a task observation and documentation

Supporting Skills

- Lists the critical steps in performing a specific task
- Estimates the difficulty of doing the task by a typical performer
- Observes and interviews a master performer while he or she does the task
- Asks basic and follow-up questions of master performers to gain an understanding of critical tasks
- Validates documentation by making a final observation

Supporting Attitudes

- Is interested in being accurate and complete in documentation

Basic Needs Assessment Competency 6: Facilitates a Feedback Meeting to Interpret Data

Interprets survey data and makes recommendations for training projects to management.

Results or Output

Recommendations

Supporting Knowledge

- Is aware of pre-survey opinions of training program sponsors and supervisors

Supporting Skills

- Analyzes data
- Asks appropriate questions
- Makes recommendations based on survey data

Supporting Attitude

- Is willing to justify data interpretation

Advanced Needs Assessment Competency 6: Facilitates a Feedback Meeting to Interpret Data

Conducts a feedback meeting with training program sponsors and supervisors to interpret survey data and gain agreement on project objectives

Results or Output

Shared recommendations

Supporting Knowledge

- Is aware of how to conduct a feedback meeting
- Is aware of pre-survey opinions of training program sponsors and supervisors
- Understands survey techniques to collect and interpret statistically significant data

Supporting Skills

- Analyzes data
- Asks appropriate questions
- Encourages others to rationalize data interpretations
- Helps a group to reach consensus and support group recommendations
- Makes recommendations based on survey data and business needs

Supporting Attitudes

- Is willing to discuss alternative interpretations of data
- Is determined to encourage consensus decision making rather than forcing choices on group members

Needs Assessor Development Plan

Following the completion of a competency checklist, create a development plan that identifies the needs assessor's strengths, identifies areas for coaching and feedback, and identifies missing knowledge and skills along with resources for development. Beginning a development plan with a needs assessor's strengths acknowledges *this person's* strengths that can be built on for further development. Strengths can also be used to mentor others. Areas for coaching and feedback can be competencies that were not observed. There may be competencies that require more practice because the needs assessor may already have supporting knowledge and attitudes, but did not display the skill. Areas that are missing can be deficient because some knowledge, skills, or attitudes are missing. Refer to the secondary checklists to identify what is missing and plan what resources are available to build these competencies.

Gain agreement from management for the commitment of resources for development. Agree on a time frame for the development and reevaluation of the competency.

A sample Needs Assessor Development Plan Template is on the next page.

Needs Assessor Development Plan Template

Needs assessor's name: _____   Date: _____

   1. List competencies that exceed expectation:

   2. Identify:

Underdeveloped or Unobserved Competencies	Knowledge, Skills, and Attitudes to Acquire

   3. Identify competencies that require coaching and feedback:

   4. Identify resources required to develop these competencies:

Target date for re-evaluation: _____
_____

Training Needs Assessment. Copyright © 2006 by Jean Barbazette. Reproduced by permission of Pfeiffer, an Imprint of Wiley. www.pfeiffer.com

Competencies for Training Planners

Basic Planning Competency 1: Identifies the Training Issue and How It Relates to a Business Need

Training needs are explored, training issues extracted and documented. A training plan is written that provides solutions to the problems brought to the training organization.

Results or Output

Training plan

Supporting Knowledge

- Is aware of the difference between issues, problems, and needs
- Is aware of the difference between symptoms and problems

Supporting Skills

- Creates a problem statement that is related to a training request
- Identifies how the solution of the problem can be resolved by training

Supporting Attitudes

- Is willing to raise and distinguish training needs from non-training issues

---

[1]The material in this section is largely taken from the first book in this series by Jean Barbazette: *The Trainer's Journey to Competence*. San Francisco: Pfeiffer. Used with permission.

Advanced Planning Competency 1: Identifies the Training Issue and How It Relates to a Business Need

Organizational issues and business needs are explored, training issues extracted and documented. A training plan is written that provides solutions to the problems.

Results or Output

Training plan

Supporting Knowledge

- Is aware of business needs and their origins
- Is aware of the difference between issues, problems, and needs
- Is aware of the difference between symptoms and problems

Supporting Skills

- Creates a problem statement that is related to a business need
- Identifies a variety of solutions to the problem
- Only recommends a training solution when the problem can be appropriately resolved by training
- Identifies non-training problems and recommends alternative solutions

Supporting Attitudes

- Is willing to raise and distinguish training needs from non-training issues
- Is interested in the deeper or root causes of issues or problems

Basic Planning Competency 2: States the Outcome, Results, and Objectives of the Training

Given a training issue, identifies whether the requested training is justified by the rationale from the person who requests the training.

Results or Output

Training event rationale

Supporting Knowledge

- Is aware of how to justify training needs
- Is aware of the desired results that could come from training solutions

Supporting Skills

- Uses specific, descriptive language to justify the requested training event
- Writes objectives for training request

Supporting Attitude

- Is helpful

Advanced Planning Competency 2: States the Outcome, Results, and Objectives of the Training

Given a training issue that is related to a business need, identifies the desired outcome or results and the objective of the training to meet the business need.

Results or Output

Training plan

Supporting Knowledge

- Is aware of business needs and their origins
- Is aware of the desired results that could come from training solutions

Supporting Skills

- Uses specific, descriptive language to identify the desired outcome or results
- Writes objectives for training that will meet a business need

Supporting Attitude

- Is willing to adapt a focus for a project beyond a training component

Basic Planning Competency 3: States the Performance Deficiency and Its Causes

Identifies the performance deficiency and its causes that are related to the proposed training event.

Results or Output

Training event justification

Supporting Knowledge

- Understands what causes performance deficiencies
- Understands how to fix performance deficiencies

Supporting Skills

- Describes performance deficiencies in an objective manner
- Describes the various types of causes for performance deficiencies

Supporting Attitudes

- Is open-minded
- Is objective

Advanced Planning Competency 3: States the Performance Deficiency and Its Causes

Identifies the performance deficiency and its causes that are related to the business need and the proposed training.

Results or Output

Performance deficiencies and causes

Supporting Knowledge

- Is aware of how the business works
- Understands what causes performance deficiencies
- Understands how to fix performance deficiencies

Supporting Skills

- Describes performance deficiencies in an objective manner
- Describes the various types of causes for performance deficiencies

Supporting Attitudes

- Is open-minded
- Is objective
- Is interested in the deeper or root causes of issues or problems

Basic Planning Competency 4: Identifies or Establishes Performance Standards

Identifies existing performance standards for tasks that are performed deficiently. Where no standards exist, the course designer requests that the operations supervisor or manager establish performance standards.

Results or Output

Performance standards

Supporting Knowledge

- Is aware of existing performance standards
- Is aware of lines of authority for establishing performance standards

Supporting Skills

- Cites existing standards that are not being met by how the job is done currently
- If no standards exist, requests that the operations supervisor or manager establish performance standards

Supporting Attitudes

- Is flexible
- Is determined to develop a useful work product given an approved format

Advanced Planning Competency 4: Identifies or Establishes Performance Standards

Identify existing performance standards for tasks that are performed deficiently. Where no standards exist, collaborates with subject-matter experts to establish performance standards.

Results or Output

Performance standards

Supporting Knowledge

- Is aware of existing performance standards
- Understands how to collaboratively establish performance standards

Supporting Skills

- Cites existing standards that are not being met by how the job is done currently
- If no standards exist, collaborates with subject-matter experts to establish performance standards in an approved format

Supporting Attitudes

- Is flexible
- Is determined to develop a useful work product, given an approved format

Basic Planning Competency 5: Identifies the Target Population

Based on prior analysis, identifies the target population for this training project.

Results or Output

Target population statement

Supporting Knowledge

- Is aware of which people/employees constitute the target population
- Understands some of the decisions that will be made based on the data collected

Supporting Skills

- Asks appropriate questions
- Interviews a sufficient number of the target population to make appropriate recommendations
- Recommends content and grouping of the target population for the training

Supporting Attitudes

- Is sensitive to the needs of the target population

Advanced Planning Competency 5: Identifies the Target Population

Based on prior analysis, identifies the target population for this training project.

Results or Output

Target population statement

Supporting Knowledge

- Is aware of which people/employees constitute the target population
- Is aware of different types of information to seek about the target population
- Understands the decisions that will be made based on the data collected
- Understands what constitutes appropriate questions for a specific target population

Supporting Skills

- Asks appropriate questions
- Interviews a sufficient number of the target population to make appropriate recommendations
- Collects information through surveys when appropriate
- Writes justifications for content selection and grouping decisions based on the data

Supporting Attitudes

- Is sensitive to the needs of the target population
- Avoids making the target population defensive and is willing to answer questions

Basic Planning Competency 6: Establishes Criteria to Evaluate the Training

Identifies how the participant reaction and learning will be evaluated.

Results or Output

Evaluation tools

Supporting Knowledge

- Is aware of the reaction sheets
- Is aware of testing methods

Supporting Skills

- Identifies how to customize the reaction sheet for this training event
- Identifies ways to measure participant learning

Supporting Attitude

- Fairness in testing

Advanced Planning Competency 6: Establish Criteria to Evaluate the Training

Identifies and gains agreement from the target population's manager for how the training project will be evaluated and which of the four levels of evaluation are appropriate for this project.

Results or Output

Evaluation tools

Supporting Knowledge

- Is aware of the four levels of evaluation

Supporting Skills

- Selects the appropriate levels of evaluation for this project

Supporting Attitude

- Flexibility

Basic Planning Competency 7: Describes the Proposed Intervention

Describes the training event that will meet the need in the training plan objectives.

Results or Output

Training event description

Supporting Knowledge

- Understands what makes training effective
- Understands the cause-and-effect relationship of sequencing training activities

Supporting Skills

- Creates a content outline and learning objectives
- Describes the rationale for the sequence of training activities

Supporting Attitude

- Is interested in influencing the client

Advanced Planning Competency 7: Describes the Proposed Intervention

Describes the variety of activities in the appropriate sequence to address the need in the training plan objectives.

Results or Output

Variety of activities and interventions, job aids

Supporting Knowledge

- Understands which types of activities are suited to specific objectives
- Understands the cause-and-effect relationship of sequencing project activities

Supporting Skills

- Lists the proposed activities (training, job aids, coaching, new policy, and so forth) for the project
- Describes the rationale for the sequence of activities

Supporting Attitude

- Is willing to provide enough detail to make the intervention understood

Basic Planning Competency 8: Estimates the Cost of the Training Plan

Lists the anticipated expenses to conduct the training event.

Results or Output

Estimated costs

Supporting Knowledge

- Understands cost-collection techniques

Supporting Skills

- Estimates training expenses to design and present the training event

Supporting Attitudes

- Is willing to reveal true costs

Advanced Planning Competency 8: Estimates the Cost of the Training Plan

Lists the direct and indirect expenses to implement the training plan. Describes the cost of current performance. Compares current performance cost with the estimated cost of doing the training.

Results or Output

Feasibility cost estimate

Supporting Knowledge

- Understands cost estimation
- Understands methods of cost comparison

Supporting Skills

- Shows the cost of current performance, the cost of an implemented training plan, and when to expect a return on the training investment
- Distinguishes between direct and indirect expenses

Supporting Attitude

- Is willing to reveal true costs

Basic Planning Competency 9: Builds a Partnership with Management to Ensure Success of the Training Plan

Creates and delivers to supervisors and managers an announcement of the training event, along with a description of the course content and learning objectives.

Results or Output

Training announcement

Supporting Knowledge

- Understands effective course announcements

Supporting Skills

- Produces a course announcement in a timely manner

Supporting Attitude

- Desires clarity and accuracy of course announcement

Advanced Planning Competency 9: Builds a Partnership with Management to Ensure Success of the Training Plan

Partners with supervisors, managers, and learners before, during, and after the proposed training plan is carried out.

Results or Output

Partnership roles

Supporting Knowledge

- Is aware of appropriate partnership strategies for each phase of the project
- Understands the role of self and others in partnering on a training project

Supporting Skills

- Develops a partnership plan to gain the support of management and the target population for the training project
- Produces information and materials to support the training project

Supporting Attitude

- Is willing to go beyond the presentation of a training event to make a training project successful

Basic Planning Competency 10: Schedules Training

Proposes a training schedule to attract maximum attendance from the target population.

Results or Output

Training schedule

Supporting Knowledge

- Is aware of organization's holidays
- Is aware of trainers' expertise in recommending trainers to teach classes

Supporting Skills

- Sets an optimum schedule of training classes according to trainer availability
- Resolves scheduling conflicts for trainers

Supporting Attitude

- Is willing to negotiate with trainers to create an optimum schedule

Advanced Planning Competency 10: Schedules Training

Proposes a training schedule to attract maximum attendance from the target population. Resolves conflicts between the training schedule and the needs of the business.

Results or Output

Training schedule

Supporting Knowledge

- Understands how a training schedule can impact business needs
- Is aware of organization's holidays
- Is aware of trainers' expertise in recommending trainers to teach classes

Supporting Skills

- Sets an optimum schedule of training classes
- Resolves scheduling conflicts

Supporting Attitude

- Is willing to negotiate with trainers, supervisors, and trainees to create an optimum schedule

Training Planner Development Plan

Following the completion of a competency checklist, create a development plan that identifies the training planner's strengths, identifies areas for coaching and feedback, and identifies missing knowledge and skills along with resources for development. Beginning a development plan with a training planner's strengths acknowledges this person's strengths that can be built on for further development. Strengths can also be used to mentor others. Areas for coaching and feedback can be competencies that were not observed. There may be competencies that require more practice because the training planner may already have supporting knowledge and attitudes, but did not display the skill. Areas that are missing can be deficient because some knowledge, skills, or attitudes are missing. Refer to the secondary checklists to identify what is missing and plan what resources are available to build these competencies.

Gain agreement from management for the commitment of resources for development. Agree on a time frame for the development and reevaluation of the competency.

A sample Training Planner Development Plan Template is on the next page.

Training Planner Development Plan Template

Training planner's name: _____ Date: _____

1. List competencies that exceed expectation: _____

    _____

    _____

    _____

    _____

2. Identify:

Underdeveloped or Unobserved Competencies	Knowledge, Skills, and Attitudes to Acquire

3. Identify competencies that require coaching and feedback: _____

    _____

    _____

    _____

    _____

4. Identify resources required to develop these competencies: _____

    _____

    _____

    _____

Target date for re-evaluation: _____

Competency. An observable behavior supported by specific knowledge, skills, and attitudes. Each competency has specific results or output.

Competency model. A set of competencies for a specific role. Shows optimum behaviors with supporting knowledge, skills, and attitudes for a specific role, such as needs assessor or training plan developer.

Contextual analysis. Takes information from other analyses and answers how, when, and where training will be delivered. It compares different delivery mediums and addresses scheduling issues and other logistics.

Cost/benefit analysis. An estimate of the cost of the training weighed against the possible benefits of training.

Course designer. A person who designs a training program based on a needs assessment and a training plan and includes writing learning objectives, creating learning activities, lesson plans, and audiovisuals.

Development plan. Suggests ways to correct a deficiency to meet a goal.

Evaluation criteria. A list of behaviors that are met in order to describe achievement or success.

Feasibility analysis. A cost/benefit analysis completed prior to conducting training. It is an estimate of the cost of the training weighed against the possible benefits that could be achieved if training were conducted. A feasibility analysis identifies whether conducting the training costs less than doing nothing.

Feedback meeting. Also called a debrief meeting, where the needs assessor tells decision makers what information or data have been collected. Data are interpreted and recommendations created and become part of the training plan.

"Gap" analysis. Also called performance analysis; identifies the difference between current performance and the desired performance.

Goal analysis. A consensus process to make a vague desire more specific and measurable.

Intervention. An activity to improve performance.

Interview. The process of asking questions of experts or performers to identify training needs.

Job analysis. The process of identifying all the parts of a specific job; conducted before conducting a task analysis.

Learning objective. Describes specific behavior, conditions, level of achievement and is written from the learner's point of view.

Needs assessment. Gathering of information about a specific business need that can be resolved by training. The many types of needs assessments include performance analysis, target population analysis, sorting training needs and wants, job analysis, and task analysis.

"Needs versus wants" analysis. Discovers training needs that are related to the organization's business. Training is linked to the bottom line and providing appropriate training will benefit the individual as well as the organization.

Participant learning hour (PLH). Calculated by multiplying the number of participants by class hours. PLH is later divided into the total cost to get the cost per participant and cost per learning hour. The cost per learning hour, similar to a "man hour" figure, can be used to compare the cost of one training program to another.

Performance analysis. Also known as "gap" analysis. Performance analysis looks at an employee's current performance and identifies whether or not an employee is performing as desired.

Performance deficiency. A difference with a negative connotation, implying that the employee is not meeting a known standard for performance.

Performance standards. An implied or explicit desired level for minimum performance.

Post-training analysis. Occurs after training has been completed and attempts to identify the cause of continuing deficient performance.

Skill deficiency. When a task is not being done correctly due to a lack of skill by the performer.

Skill hierarchy. An arrangement of skills that shows dependence of one skill on another. A graphic representation of the skills *any learner* must possess in order to meet the learning objective. It looks like an organization chart because it shows the *relationship* between skills. The hierarchy is not specific to a particular learner; it is specific to the task.

Target population. The individuals or group involved in a needs assessment or training program.

Target population analysis. Collects information about who will attend the training. The results of a target population analysis yield two types of information: first, it helps you decide who needs training and how a specific course must be customized to meet the participants' needs, and second, what class groupings are appropriate.

Task analysis. Finds the best method and sequence of steps to complete a specific task.

Trainer. This person presents information and directs structured learning experiences so individuals increase their knowledge and skills. This person can also act as a performance coach and facilitator.

Training needs assessment. The process of collecting information about an expressed or implied organizational need that could be met by conducting training.

Training plan. Based on a needs assessment, a training plan identifies training issues, recommends results and objectives, and suggests how they can be reached. The plan states the causes of a deficiency, what performance standards are not being met, and who is the target population. The plan further recommends a means to evaluate suggested strategies, how to partner with management, and when interventions are to be scheduled.

Training program. A training course or event to improve the knowledge, skills, and attitudes of employees to meet a business need.

BIBLIOGRAPHY

Aho, Kaye, and Frantzreb, Richard B. "Be a Better Job Analyst." *ASTD Info-Line*, March 1989.

Barbazette, Jean. *Instant Case Studies*. San Francisco: Pfeiffer, 2003.

Barbazette, Jean, *The Trainer's Journey to Competence: Tools, Assessments and Models*. San Francisco: Pfeiffer, 2005.

Barksdale, Susan, and Murdock, Mike. *Rapid Needs Analysis*. Alexandria, VA American Society for Training and Development, 2001.

Biech, Elaine. *Training for Dummies*. New York: John Wiley & Sons, 2005.

Brethower, Dale, and Smalley, Karolyn. *Performance-Based Instruction: Linking Training to Business Results*. San Francisco: Pfeiffer, 1998.

Carkhuff, Robert, and Fisher, Sharon. *Instructional Systems Design*. Amherst, MA: HRD Press, 1983.

Chapnick, Samantha. "Needs Assessment for E-Learning." *ASTD Info-Line*, December 2000.

Conway, Malcolm. "How to Measure Customer Satisfaction." *ASTD Info-Line*, January 2000.

Conway, Malcolm. "Collecting Data with Electronic Tools." *ASTD Info-Line*, April 2004.

Creative Research Systems. *Statistical Significance*. www.surveysystem.com/signif.htm.

Fisher, Sharon, and Ruffino, Barbara. *Establishing the Value of Training*. Amherst, MA: HRD Press, 1996.

Fletcher, Shirley. *Competency-Based Assessment Techniques*. London: Kogan Page, 2001.

Ford, Donald J. *Bottom-Line Training*. Houston, TX: Gulf, 1999.

Gagne, Robert M., and others. *Principles of Instructional Design* (5th ed.). Belmont, CA: Wadsworth, 2005.

Gilly, Jerry W. "How to Collect Data." *ASTD Info-Line*, August 1980.

Gupta, Kavita. "Conducting a Mini Needs Assessment." *ASTD Info-Line*, November 1996.

Gupta, Kavita. *A Practical Guide to Needs Assessment*. San Francisco: Pfeiffer, 1999.

Holcomb, Jane. *Training Evaluation Made Easy: Make Your Training Worth Every Penny.* London: Kogan Page, 1998.

Jonassen, Wallace H. *Task Analysis Methods for Instructional Design.* Mahwah, NJ: Lawrence Erlbaum & Associates, 1999.

Long, Lori. "Surveys from Start to Finish." *ASTD Info-Line,* December 1986.

Mager, Robert F., and Beach, Kenneth M. Jr. *Developing Vocational Instruction.* Atlanta, GA: Center for Effective Performance, 1967.

Mager, Robert F., and Pipe, Peter. *Analyzing Performance Problems: Or You Really Oughta Wanna.* Atlanta, GA: Center for Effective Performance, 1997.

McArdle, Geri. *Conducting a Needs Analysis* Palo Alto, CA: Crisp, 1998.

McConnell, John H. *How to Identify Your Organization's Training Needs: A Practical Guide to Needs Analysis.* New York: AMACOM, 2003.

McCoy, Carol P. *Managing the Small Training Staff.* Alexandria, VA: American Society for Training and Development, 1998.

Motulsky, Harvey. "Prism Guide to Interpreting Statistical Results." *Analyzing Data with GraphPad Prism.* San Diego, CA: GraphPad Software, 1999.

Parry, Scott. *The Training House Assessment Kit.* Princeton, NJ: Training House, 2000.

Parry, Scott. *Training for Results.* Alexandria, VA: American Society for Training and Development, 2000.

Peterson, Robyn. *Training Needs Assessment.* London: Kogan Page, 1998.

Phillips, Jack J. *In Action: Conducting Needs Assessments.* Alexandria, VA: American Society for Training and Development, 1995.

Robinson, Dana Gaines, and Robinson, James C. *Training for Impact: How to Link Training to Business Needs and Measure the Results.* San Francisco: Jossey-Bass, 1989.

Rossett, Allison. *First Things Fast.* San Francisco: Pfeiffer, 1999.

Silberman, Mel. *The Consultant's Big Book of Reproducible Surveys and Questionnaires.* New York: McGraw-Hill, 2003.

Sparhawk, Sally. *Identifying Targeted Training Needs.* San Francisco: Pfeiffer, 1999.

Sparhawk, Sally, and Schickling, Marian. "Strategic Needs Analysis." *ASTD Info-Line,* August 1994.

Thompson, Bruce. "The Concept of Statistical Significance Testing." *Practical Assessment, Research & Evaluation,* 1999. http://pareonline.net.

Waagen, Alice K. "Task Analysis." *ASTD Info-Line,* August 1998.

Zemke, Ron, and Rossett, Allison. "Be a Better Needs Analyst," *ASTD Info-Line,* February 1985.

Zemke, Ron, and Kramlinger, Thomas. *Figuring Things Out: A Trainer's Guide to Needs and Task Analysis.* Reading, MA: Addison-Wesley, 1982.

INDEX

Jean Barbazette is the president of The Training Clinic, a training and consulting firm she founded in 1977. Her company focuses on training trainers throughout the United States for major profit, non-profit, and government organizations. The Training Clinic has three international licensees in the Netherlands, Hungary, and Colombia. Prior books include *Successful New Employee Orientation* (2nd ed.) (Pfeiffer, 2001); *The Trainer's Support Handbook* (McGraw-Hill, 2001); *Instant Case Studies* (Pfeiffer, 2003), and *The Trainer's Journey to Competence* (Pfeiffer, 2005). She is a frequent contributor to *ASTD Training & Development Sourcebooks*, *McGraw-Hill Training & Performance Sourcebooks*, and *Pfeiffer Annuals*.

Jean Barbazette, President
The Training Clinic
645 Seabreeze Drive
Seal Beach, CA 90740
jean@thetrainingclinic.com
www.thetrainingclinic.com

System Requirements

PC with Microsoft Windows 98SE or later

Mac with Apple OS version 8.6 or later

Using the CD with Windows

To view the items located on the CD, follow these steps:

1. Insert the CD into your computer's CD-ROM drive.

2. A window appears with the following options:

    Contents: Allows you to view the files included on the CD-ROM.

    Software: Allows you to install useful software from the CD-ROM.

    Links: Displays a hyperlinked page of websites.

    Author: Displays a page with information about the author(s).

    Contact Us: Displays a page with information on contacting the publisher or author.

    Help: Displays a page with information on using the CD.

    Exit: Closes the interface window.

If you do not have autorun enabled, or if the autorun window does not appear, follow these steps to access the CD:

1. Click Start→Run.

2. In the dialog box that appears, type d:start.exe, where d is the letter of your CD-ROM drive. This brings up the autorun window described in the preceding set of steps.

3. Choose the desired option from the menu. (See Step 2 in the preceding list for a description of these options.)

In Case of Trouble

If you experience difficulty using the CD-ROM, please follow these steps:

1. Make sure your hardware and systems configurations conform to the systems requirements noted under "System Requirements" above.

2. Review the installation procedure for your type of hardware and operating system.

It is possible to reinstall the software if necessary.

To speak with someone in Product Technical Support, call 800-762-2974 or 317-572-3994 M-F 8:30 a.m.-5:00 p.m. EST. You can also get support and contact Product Technical Support through our website at www.wiley.com/ techsupport.

Before calling or writing, please have the following information available:

- Type of computer and operating system
- Any error messages displayed
- Complete description of the problem.

It is best if you are sitting at your computer when making the call.

Pfeiffer Publications Guide

This guide is designed to familiarize you with the various types of Pfeiffer publications. The formats section describes the various types of products that we publish; the methodologies section describes the many different ways that content might be provided within a product. We also provide a list of the topic areas in which we publish.

FORMATS

In addition to its extensive book-publishing program, Pfeiffer offers content in an array of formats, from fieldbooks for the practitioner to complete, ready-to-use training packages that support group learning.

FIELDBOOK Designed to provide information and guidance to practitioners in the midst of action. Most fieldbooks are companions to another, sometimes earlier, work, from which its ideas are derived; the fieldbook makes practical what was theoretical in the original text. Fieldbooks can certainly be read from cover to cover. More likely, though, you'll find yourself bouncing around following a particular theme, or dipping in as the mood, and the situation, dictates.

HANDBOOK A contributed volume of work on a single topic, comprising an eclectic mix of ideas, case studies, and best practices sourced by practitioners and experts in the field.

An editor or team of editors usually is appointed to seek out contributors and to evaluate content for relevance to the topic. Think of a handbook not as a ready-to-eat meal, but as a cookbook of ingredients that enables you to create the most fitting experience for the occasion.

RESOURCE Materials designed to support group learning. They come in many forms: a complete, ready-to-use exercise (such as a game); a comprehensive resource on one topic (such as conflict management) containing a variety of methods and approaches; or a collection of like-minded activities (such as icebreakers) on multiple subjects and situations.

TRAINING PACKAGE An entire, ready-to-use learning program that focuses on a particular topic or skill. All packages comprise a guide for the facilitator/trainer and a workbook for the participants. Some packages are supported with additional media—such as video—or learning aids, instruments, or other devices to help participants understand concepts or practice and develop skills.

- *Facilitator/trainer's guide* Contains an introduction to the program, advice on how to organize and facilitate the learning event, and step-by-step instructor notes. The guide also contains copies of presentation materials—handouts, presentations, and overhead designs, for example—used in the program.

- *Participant's workbook* Contains exercises and reading materials that support the learning goal and serves as a valuable reference and support guide for participants in the weeks and months that follow the learning event. Typically, each participant will require his or her own workbook.

ELECTRONIC CD-ROMs and web-based products transform static Pfeiffer content into dynamic, interactive experiences. Designed to take advantage of the searchability, automation, and ease-of-use that technology provides, our e-products bring convenience and immediate accessibility to your workspace.

METHODOLOGIES

CASE STUDY A presentation, in narrative form, of an actual event that has occurred inside an organization. Case studies are not prescriptive, nor are they used to prove a point; they are designed to develop critical analysis and decision-making skills. A case study has a specific time frame, specifies a sequence of events, is narrative in structure, and contains a plot structure— an issue (what should be/have been done?). Use case studies when the goal is to enable participants to apply previously learned theories to the circumstances in the case, decide what is pertinent, identify the real issues, decide what should have been done, and develop a plan of action.

ENERGIZER A short activity that develops readiness for the next session or learning event. Energizers are most commonly used after a break or lunch to stimulate or refocus the group. Many involve some form of physical activity, so they are a useful way to counter post-lunch lethargy. Other uses include transitioning from one topic to another, where "mental" distancing is important.

EXPERIENTIAL LEARNING ACTIVITY (ELA) A facilitator-led intervention that moves participants through the learning cycle from experience to application (also known as a Structured Experience). ELAs are carefully thought-out designs in which there is a definite learning purpose and intended outcome. Each step—everything that participants do during the activity—facilitates the accomplishment of the stated goal. Each ELA includes complete instructions for facilitating the intervention and a clear statement of goals, suggested group size and timing, materials required, an explanation of the process, and, where appropriate, possible variations to the activity. (For more detail on Experiential Learning Activities, see the Introduction to the *Reference Guide to Handbooks and Annuals*, 1999 edition, Pfeiffer, San Francisco.)

GAME A group activity that has the purpose of fostering team sprit and togetherness in addition to the achievement of a pre-stated goal. Usually contrived—undertaking a desert expedition, for example—this type of learning method offers an engaging means for participants to demonstrate and practice business and interpersonal skills. Games are effective for team-building and personal development mainly because the goal is subordinate to the process—the means through which participants reach decisions, collaborate, communicate, and generate trust and understanding. Games often engage teams in "friendly" competition.

ICEBREAKER A (usually) short activity designed to help participants overcome initial anxiety in a training session and/or to acquaint the participants with one another. An icebreaker can be a fun activity or can be tied to specific topics or training goals. While a useful tool in itself, the icebreaker comes into its own in situations where tension or resistance exists within a group.

INSTRUMENT A device used to assess, appraise, evaluate, describe, classify, and summarize various aspects of human behavior. The term used to describe an instrument depends primarily on its format and purpose. These terms include survey, questionnaire, inventory, diagnostic, survey, and poll. Some uses of instruments include providing instrumental feedback to group members, studying here-and-now processes or functioning within a group, manipulating group composition, and evaluating outcomes of training and other interventions.

Instruments are popular in the training and HR field because, in general, more growth can occur if an individual is provided with a method for focusing specifically on his or her own behavior. Instruments also are used to obtain information that will serve as a basis for change and to assist in workforce planning efforts.

Paper-and-pencil tests still dominate the instrument landscape with a typical package comprising a facilitator's guide, which offers advice on administering the instrument and interpreting the collected data, and an initial set of instruments. Additional instruments are available separately. Pfeiffer, though, is investing heavily in e-instruments. Electronic instrumentation provides effortless distribution and, for larger groups particularly, offers advantages over paper-and-pencil tests in the time it takes to analyze data and provide feedback.

LECTURETTE A short talk that provides an explanation of a principle, model, or process that is pertinent to the participants' current learning needs. A lecturette is intended to establish a common language bond between the trainer and the participants by providing a mutual frame of reference. Use a lecturette as an introduction to a group activity or event, as an interjection during an event, or as a handout.

MODEL A graphic depiction of a system or process and the relationship among its elements. Models provide a frame of reference and something more tangible, and more easily remembered, than a verbal explanation. They also give participants something to "go on," enabling them to track their own progress as they experience the dynamics, processes, and relationships being depicted in the model.

ROLE PLAY A technique in which people assume a role in a situation/scenario: a customer service rep in an angry-customer exchange, for example. The way in which the role is approached is then discussed and feedback is offered. The role play is often repeated using a different approach and/or incorporating changes made based on feedback received. In other words, role playing is a spontaneous interaction involving realistic behavior under artificial (and safe) conditions.

SIMULATION A methodology for understanding the interrelationships among components of a system or process. Simulations differ from games in that they test or use a model that depicts or mirrors some aspect of reality in form, if not necessarily in content. Learning occurs by studying the effects of change on one or more factors of the model. Simulations are commonly used to test hypotheses about what happens in a system—often referred to as "what if?" analysis—or to examine best-case/worst-case scenarios.

THEORY A presentation of an idea from a conjectural perspective. Theories are useful because they encourage us to examine behavior and phenomena through a different lens.

TOPICS

The twin goals of providing effective and practical solutions for workforce training and organization development and meeting the educational needs of training and human resource professionals shape Pfeiffer's publishing program. Core topics include the following:

Leadership & Management

Communication & Presentation

Coaching & Mentoring

Training & Development

e-Learning

Teams & Collaboration

OD & Strategic Planning

Human Resources

Consulting

What will you find on pfeiffer.com?

- The best in workplace performance solutions for training and HR professionals
- Downloadable training tools, exercises, and content
- Web-exclusive offers
- Training tips, articles, and news
- Seamless on-line ordering
- Author guidelines, information on becoming a Pfeiffer Affiliate, and much more

Discover more at www.pfeiffer.com